VIDEO GAMES

FUTURE TECH

COMPUTER SCIENCE

---

for Curious Kids

An illustrated introduction to software programming,
artificial intelligence, cyber-security—and more!

NETWORKS

WEB DESIGN

ARCTURUS

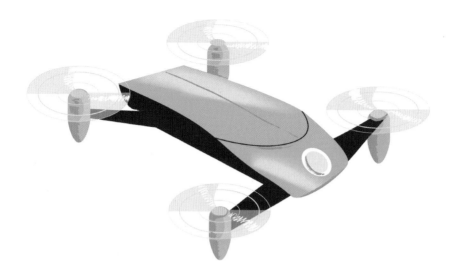

ARCTURUS

This edition published in 2024 by Arcturus Publishing Limited
26/27 Bickels Yard, 151–153 Bermondsey Street,
London SE1 3HA

Author: Chris Oxlade
Illustrator: Nik Neves
Consultant: Tom Jackson
Designer: Dani Leigh
Editors: Lydia Halliday, William Potter

ISBN: 978-1-3988-3109-4
CH010938US
Supplier 29, Date 1123, PI 00006000

Printed in China

CONTENTS

WELCOME TO THE WORLD OF COMPUTER SCIENCE

Computer science is the study of computers—what they are, how they work, and how we program them to do jobs for us. Computer science is a very important subject because computers play such a huge part in our lives. When you hear the word "computer," you might think of a laptop or a desktop computer, but smartphones, tablets, games consoles, and smart speakers are all computers, too. There are also computers hidden away in machines such as dishwashers, cars, planes, and even toys.

In this book, you'll discover when the first computers were invented, and learn about the different parts of a modern computer and how they store and process information. You'll find out about programming skills and languages such as Python and Scratch, which can make computers do a wide range of tasks. You'll also learn about the ways in which computers communicate with each other across the world via the Internet and how they help keep the world running.

CHAPTER 1

THE HISTORY OF COMPUTING

Our modern world is full of computers. You can find them in homes, schools, stores, and factories. Most of us carry a computer around with us every day—a smartphone is a handheld computer. We rely on the Internet (a vast network of computers) for finding things out, for entertainment, shopping, and booking vacations.

In this chapter, we will find out about the history of computers and the Internet. The kind of computers you might recognize today, with keyboards and screens, appeared about 50 years ago. But the timeline of computers is a long one that began thousands of years ago with simple mechanical calculating machines.

MECHANICAL CALCULATORS

Modern electronic computers, designed to do complicated mathematical calculations at high speed, are a twentieth-century invention. However, the history of computers started thousands of years earlier with the invention of simple mechanical calculators, such as the abacus, which was used by traders to keep track of their money.

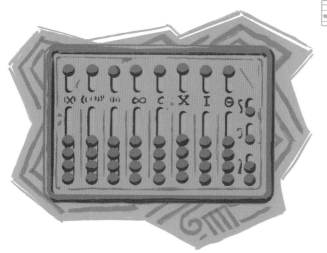

ADDING WITH BEADS

The **abacus** is one of the oldest calculating devices known. We don't know exactly when or where the abacus was invented, but it was probably more than 3,000 years ago in Babylonia. On an abacus, numbers are represented by the position of beads in grooves or on wires. Calculations are done by moving the beads one way or the other (to add or subtract). Over hundreds of years, knowledge of the abacus spread to Asia and Europe. This example comes from ancient Rome.

NUMBER STICKS

In the early seventeenth century, Scottish mathematician John Napier invented a simple set of numbered wooden rods known as **Napier's bones**. The rods were designed to make it easy to multiply large numbers. In a set of Napier's bones, there is a rod for each digit from one to nine with a times table engraved on it. The rods are placed next to each other in a frame to do multiplication.

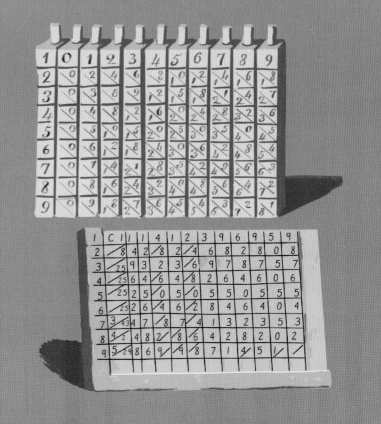

COG CALCULATING

In 1642, French mathematician Blaise Pascal invented a machine that used a complex system of cogs to add and subtract automatically. The machine is known as the **Pascaline calculator**. Calculations were done by setting numbers on the wheels and turning them to add or subtract. The cogs inside the box carried numbers to the next column, and the results were shown by digits in small windows.

PROGRAMMABLE MACHINERY

Computers are programmable machines—different **programs** make a computer do different jobs for us. The idea of programming a machine was developed more than 200 years ago by Frenchman Joseph Marie Jacquard. He built a loom that was programmed to weave different patterns in cloth. The program for a pattern was contained on sheets of "punch" cards. The pattern of holes on the cards controlled the pattern woven by the loom.

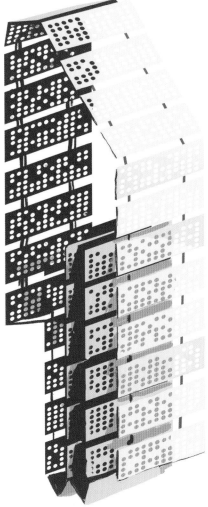

THE FIRST COMPUTERS

The first computer was a giant mechanical calculator with hundreds of cogs. It was designed by nineteenth-century British mathematician Charles Babbage, who planned to program it to do automatic calculations. However, the machine was never completed.

CALCULATING COGS

The first machine that Charles Babbage invented was called the difference engine. This was like a complex calculator. It was designed to calculate and print the detailed mathematical tables used by engineers and navigators. On completion, the machine would have contained hundreds of cogs, but the full engine was never built.

Babbage went on to design his analytical engine, which was a mechanical computer. The main part of the machine would have been the "mill," which was like the processor in a modern computer.

CHARLES BABBAGE

Charles Babbage was a British mathematician and inventor. He worked as a professor at Cambridge University. In 1823, he was given a government grant to design a machine he called a difference engine. It was one of the most complicated machines ever designed and proved impossible to build at the time. In the 1830s, Babbage abandoned the difference engine to work on the more advanced analytical engine. Although neither machine was constructed in his lifetime, Babbage's ideas were a very important step in computing history.

THE FIRST PROGRAMMER

One of Babbage's friends, Ada Lovelace, who was also a mathematician, studied the designs for the analytical engine. She worked out how to program the machine to perform complex calculations. She compared the machine to the Jacquard loom, since it would also have been programmed with punch cards. Ada Lovelace is now thought of as the world's first programmer. The ADA programming language was named after her.

ADDING MACHINES

Although Charles Babbage's machines were too advanced to be built at the time, more simple mechanical calculating machines called **adding machines** became popular from the late nineteenth century. They could be found in accounting offices until electronic calculators arrived in the 1970s. This example is a Burroughs machine, which was first developed in 1888. It has a keyboard to input numbers, and a printer to record results.

OUT OF CURIOSITY

Babbage's analytical engine was designed with enough memory space to store 1,000 numbers, each with 50 digits. This was more storage than the first electronic computers that were built 100 years later.

SWITCHING TO ELECTRICITY

A big breakthrough in the history of computers came in the 1940s. This was when it became possible to build electronic circuits to replace the cogs and levers of mechanical machines. In electronic machines, a flow of electricity could represent numbers.

ELECTROMECHANICS

Early electronic computers, such as the Harvard Mk I of 1943, had mechanical moving parts, such as relays, which used electromagnets to operate switches. These computers were known as **electromechanical** computers. The Harvard Mk I was huge and slow—it was more than 15 m (49 ft) long, weighed 5 tonnes (5.5 tons), and took several seconds to add two numbers. Later Harvard machines contained more electronic parts and fewer mechanical parts.

CODE BREAKING

In 1940, during World War II, British mathematician Alan Turing helped build an electromechanical computer called the Bombe. The machine was designed to decipher codes produced by the German Enigma code-making machine. It helped the Allies to find out what the German forces were planning. In the 1930s, Turing described a **theoretical** machine that could do the job of a modern computer, now known as a Turing machine.

PROGRAMMING WITH WIRES

The first all-electronic computer (one that had no moving mechanical parts) was the ENIAC, which was completed in 1946 in the United States. ENIAC stands for Electronic Numerical Integrator and Computer. It was the world's first general-purpose **digital** computer, although it was originally designed for calculating how far artillery shells would travel before landing. ENIAC had no keyboard or screen—it was programmed by plugging hundreds of wires into different sockets.

VACUUM TUBES

Modern computers contain millions of microscopic electronic switches embedded in **microchips**. The main reason that early electronic computers were so large is that they used thousands of **vacuum tubes** as switches. Air was pumped out of the tubes to create a vacuum, allowing beams of electrons to flow inside. The tubes were not very reliable and often needed to be replaced.

OUT OF CURIOSITY

The ENIAC computer contained 17,000 vacuum tubes and 1,500 relays. It could do 5,000 calculations per second. Some of its results were used in the development of the first hydrogen bomb.

BIG IRON

In the 1950s, people realized that computers could do many of the repetitive jobs performed for business and industry, and so the first computer manufacturing companies were born. The first commercial computers were still large machines, often known as "Big Iron."

 OFFICE MACHINES

"Big Iron" machines were hugely expensive. In the 1950s and 1960s, only the biggest companies and organizations could afford them. The computers did jobs such as recording sales figures, employee salaries, and calculating accounts. This example is a commercial computer called the UNIVAC. It took a whole team of engineers to program these machines and keep them running.

PROGRAMMING WITH HOLES

Punch cards were still a common way of programming early computers. The program instructions were typed into a machine that turned them into a code in the form of holes punched into cards. Each line of code needed a line of holes on the card. When the program was needed, the cards for it were fed into a card-reading machine. There may have been hundreds or thousands of cards for a single program and the **data** the program needed.

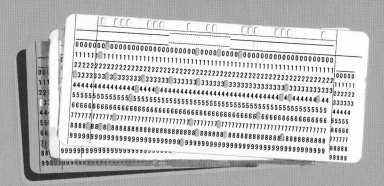

TAPE REELS

In the mid-twentieth century, there were no hard drives, memory cards, or memory sticks. Data was stored on giant reels of magnetic tape. The data was recorded in patterns in the magnetic coating on the tape. The storage capacity was low—a reel of tape could store about one **megabyte** of data—about the same needed to store just one low-resolution photo. Tapes were loaded into tape machines to be recorded on or read. Tape storage is still used today for backing up data.

MINI MACHINES

In the 1960s, smaller, cheaper versions of the "Big Iron" machines became available. These machines were known as minicomputers, although they were still bulky compared to modern personal computers. These computers made use of newly invented microchips. They were more practical for office use than earlier, larger machines. This example of a minicomputer is a popular machine called the PDP-11 from 1970. It featured a keyboard and a screen.

GOING MICRO

The 1970s and 1980s saw computers getting smaller and smaller, and cheap enough that the general public could afford them. These small machines became known as personal computers (PCs). The small size was made possible by the development of the microprocessor—a processor on a single microchip that took the place of a large set of chips in earlier machines.

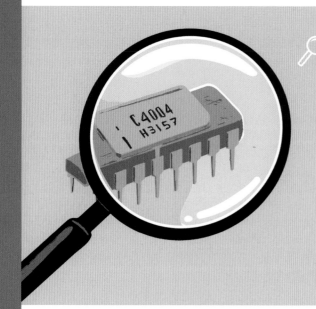

MICRO BREAKTHROUGH

A **microprocessor** (or central processing unit) is the "brains" of a personal computer. Adding **memory** and a few other components to a microprocessor completes a basic computer. The first microprocessor was the Intel 4004, built in the United States in 1971. This tiny chip, about the size of a fingernail, had the same power as a room-sized computer from the 1940s. The chip itself is hidden away inside a casing. The legs are the connections that link the chip to memory chips and other parts of the computer.

THE IBM PC

By the late 1970s and early 1980s, computers were beginning to look like the desktop machines that we would recognize today. One of the first of these computers was built by the US company IBM (International Business Machines). It featured floppy disk drives, a small screen, and a keyboard. The IBM PC and similar machines became popular in offices for simple office tasks, such as **word processing** and preparing **spreadsheets**.

THE HOME REVOLUTION

In the early 1980s, small, cheap computers for hobbyists to use at home became popular. These machines had to be programmed by the user, usually in a programming language called BASIC (short for Beginners All-Purpose Symbolic Instruction Code). One of the first was the Sinclair ZX-80, released in 1980. The ZX-80 was developed by home electronics entrepreneur Clive Sinclair. Home computers plugged into a domestic television, and games could be bought on cassette tapes.

OUT OF CURIOSITY

Early home computers had very little memory, since memory was very expensive at the time. The ZX-80 had just one kilobyte. Only small programs could be stored.

MICROSOFT

Microsoft began life in 1975, when two friends, Bill Gates and Paul Allen, began writing software for PCs. In 1980, they produced **operating software** called MS-DOS (Microsoft Disk Operating System) for IBM. MS-DOS was included with most personal computers at the time, which made huge amounts of money for Microsoft. The Microsoft Corporation now develops and sells Windows operating systems and the Office suite of programs.

HANDHELD MACHINES

The size and power of microchips continued to increase through the 1980s and 1990s. The technology of batteries and screens improved, too. It became possible to build computer-like devices small enough to be carried around. These handheld devices developed into the smartphones and tablets we use today.

PORTABLE DIGITAL ASSISTANTS

A portable digital assistant was a tiny computer, but without the power and memory of a standard PC. PDAs were like handheld personal organizers— they stored names and addresses, had a calendar, sent and received emails, took notes, and ran other simple **apps**, such as spreadsheets. The first PDA was Apple's Newton MessagePad of 1993. This is the USRobotics PalmPilot of 1997.

MUSIC PLAYERS

Digital music players were introduced in the late 1990s. At first, they were known as MP3 players because they played music files in the MP3 format. As MP3 players became more popular, memory capacity increased, so that they could store hundreds or thousands of music tracks. Small screens allowed users to select and play songs. MP3 players, such as Apple's iPod, were popular before cheaper smartphones with music-playing apps became available.

THE FIRST SMARTPHONES

In the early 2000s, manufacturers began to design phones that were a combination of a phone and a personal digital assistant. Touchscreens were not available, so the phones needed a keyboard for inputting text. They were quite large compared to today's smartphones and were too big to fit inside a pocket. Over the next few years, these phones developed into the smartphones that we recognize, which are tiny computers with touch-sensitive screens.

TABLETS

A tablet computer is a really a personal computer with a touchscreen, rather than a physical keyboard. The idea of the tablet was first thought up in the 1970s by Alan Kay, an American computer scientist, but the technology needed to build one was not available at the time. The first tablet, made by Fujitsu, was launched in 1994, but it was not until Apple introduced its first iPad in 2010 that tablets started to become popular.

GAMES CONSOLES

Games consoles are computers dedicated to playing games. The first arcade consoles and home consoles appeared in the 1970s. The games were very simple. The power and speed of games consoles has increased ever since, allowing game graphics to become more and more realistic.

SIMPLE GAMES

A machine called the Magnavox Odyssey, from 1972, was the first commercial video game console that people could buy. It ran a very simple tennis-like game that was shown on a television screen plugged into the console. There were just three moving parts in the picture —two bats and a ball. Different games could be played by plugging in different cartridges.

ARCADE GAMES

In the 1970s, most people played their games on consoles in amusement arcades. These consoles had much better games and graphics than the home consoles of the time, since the technology was very expensive. One of the first arcade games was Pong, a tennis-like game invented by Atari. Many classic games debuted on arcade consoles in the late 1970s and early 1980s, including Asteroids, Pac-Man, and Space Invaders. These games became available on home consoles as the technology became cheaper.

HANDHELD CONSOLES

Computer technology, such as processors, memory chips, and displays, continued to improve. One important development was being able to squeeze greater **processing power** and memory into a smaller space. By the end of the 1980s, all the electronics for a basic games console could be fit into a handheld device. First to appear was the Nintendo Game Boy of 1989. Games came on plug-in modules. The screen was tiny, and the games were simple, but the Game Boy became hugely popular.

OUT OF CURIOSITY

According to computer game experts, the very first computer game was Spacewar, developed in the United States in 1962. It was a simple point-and-shoot game that worked on one of the giant commercial computers of the time.

POPULAR GAMES

During the history of computer games, some titles became famous for their addictive gameplay. Space Invaders, where the player defends against a fleet of alien craft, was one of the first. Minecraft, launched in 2011, is one of the latest popular games. Modern games are put together by a huge team of experts—not only programmers but also story writers, editors, set designers, fashion designers, and directors.

CHANGING TECHNOLOGY

Although modern computers work in the same way as machines did 40 or 50 years ago, computing technology has changed a huge amount during that time. New types of computers and peripherals have been invented, and computers have become more powerful.

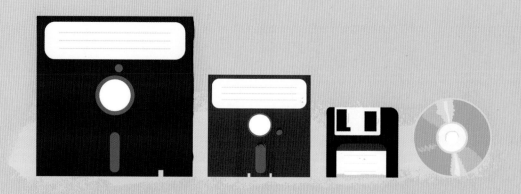

STORAGE

The way that data and programs are stored has changed completely. Early personal computers had no internal **disk drives**. Instead, system software and applications were stored on removable, flexible magnetic disks called floppy disks that were inserted into disk drives. The physical size of floppy disks gradually got smaller, but a floppy disk could only hold about a megabyte of data. Floppy drives were no longer needed after machines were made with internal hard drives. Later, software was sold and stored on CDs and DVDs, but since most **software** is now downloaded, most new machines have neither a CD nor a DVD drive.

POINTER CONTROL

Today we are used to selecting objects on-screen simply by touching them (on a touch-sensitive screen) or by clicking with a moving pointer (moved with a **trackpad**— also called a touchpad—or mouse). The first mouse was demonstrated in 1968 by American computer scientist Douglas Engelbart. It was made of wood with metal wheels that detected movement. Mice became popular when graphical user interfaces, such as Windows, were introduced in the 1980s. Trackpads have taken over from mice on laptop computers.

DESKTOP TO LAPTOP

All the early business computers and personal computers were desktop machines—all the electronics, disk drives, power supply, and other parts were in a large box that sat on a table. A monitor was placed on top of the box. There was also a keyboard and sometimes separate disk drives. The first laptop computers, such as this Osborne 1, appeared in the early 1980s. Most of the machine is made up of floppy disk drives and a tiny screen.

PROCESSOR POWER

Processors that run computers are always getting faster, so that they can perform more operations per second. This allows computers to run more and more complex software and process larger and larger files. The first processor, the Intel 4004 from 1971, had just 2,000 transistors. A modern processor might have around five billion and work through billions of calculations every second.

?

OUT OF CURIOSITY

The memory inside computers has improved dramatically. A small computer from the 1980s stored a few kilobytes of memory. A modern-day machine possesses many gigabytes—a million times more.

GROWTH OF THE INTERNET

In the 1960s, American computer scientists working for military organizations and universities decided to link their computers so that they could share the processing power of the machines. The first link was made in 1965, and gradually more computers were connected. This network of computers became known as ARPANET, and it eventually grew into the Internet.

CONNECTING WITH SOUND

When the Internet began, computers had to be connected over a telephone line using a device called an **acoustic coupler**. A telephone handset was put into the coupler. The coupler turned data signals from the computer into sound, which was picked up by the telephone and turned into a signal that went through the phone network. At the other end, the process was reversed to get the data signal back. Sending data like this was a very slow process.

EARLY EMAIL

When ARPANET (the early Internet) had been set up, the people who were using it to exchange data realized that they also could send messages to each other. In 1971, Ray Tomlinson, an American programmer, invented the first **email** system. It used the @ symbol, just like modern email addresses. People soon began using the Internet to exchange ideas as well as for sharing processing time.

INVENTING THE WEB

In 1989, British computer scientist Tim Berners-Lee was working at a research lab named CERN, in Switzerland. He came up with the idea that all the documents on CERN's computers could be organized in a logical way and linked, so that readers could jump from one document to another by clicking on words. He invented **hyperlinks**, along with **HTML**—the code for building websites, a naming system for websites, and the first-ever web browser.

SOCIAL MEDIA STARTS

In the 1990s, individuals could connect to the Internet to access websites and send emails. The use of the Internet has since grown enormously. Social media also launched in the 1990s, with blogging and bulletin boards, which allowed people to share thoughts with other people online. One of the first social media sites was Friendster, started in 2002. Facebook, the most popular social media platform in 2023, was founded in 2004.

CHAPTER 2

HARDWARE AND SOFTWARE

Computers come in many different shapes and sizes.
There are general-purpose personal computers, laptops, tablets,
smartphones, and computers hidden away inside many machines.
All these computers have similar parts and work in a similar way.

In this chapter, we look at all the parts of a personal computer,
including hardware (the physical parts of the computer) and software
(programs and data). We examine microprocessors and memory, and
see how these store and process data as **binary** numbers. We also
look at how information gets in and out of computers.

COMPUTER HARDWARE

Hardware is the name for all the physical parts of a computer. That's everything from the tiny wires that electricity travels through to the case that contains all the technology. Most computers, tablets, and phones have similar parts that make up their hardware.

POWER SUPPLY

The power supply takes power from the household electricity and sends it to the various components inside the computer. It has a transformer that reduces the voltage from the household power to the lower levels needed for the computer's parts (usually 5 or 12 volts).

MOTHERBOARD

The motherboard is a circuit board that many of the electronic parts of a computer are attached to, including the central processing unit and memory chips. The board itself is made of plastic, with metal tracks that connect the electrical components on both sides. More components plug into sockets on the motherboard.

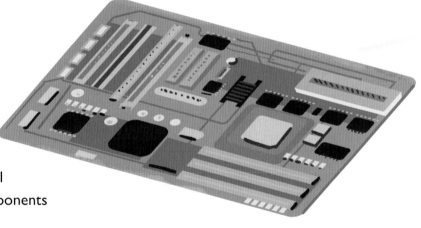

GRAPHICS CARD

Most desktop computers and laptops have a graphics card attached to the motherboard. The card contains a graphics processor and memory that is dedicated to performing the complex calculations needed to display 3D animated graphics for games and other applications.

PROCESSOR

The **central processing unit (CPU)**, or processor for short, is a computer's most complex component. It follows the instructions in a program, moves data, and makes calculations. It has dozens of **pin connections** to the tracks on the motherboard and is normally plugged into a special socket that allows it to be replaced.

MEMORY

Memory is made up of memory chips, which store programs and data. Rows of chips are mounted on small circuit boards that plug into the motherboard. Each chip contains millions of tiny circuits that each hold a binary bit of information. Most memory chips only hold data while they are powered up.

INTERNAL STORAGE

Internal storage is permanent storage for programs and data. The programs and data are loaded from here into the memory when they are needed. Internal storage can hold many times more data than memory, but it takes much longer for the data to be loaded. Internal storage can be a **hard disk drive (HDD)** or a **solid-state drive (SSD)**.

THE CPU

A central processing unit (CPU) is at the heart of every computer. It contains incredibly complicated electronic circuits. Its job is to process data following the instructions in a program. The CPU performs data calculations, sorts data, and moves it from one place to another. The processor understands a computer language called machine code that stores instructions.

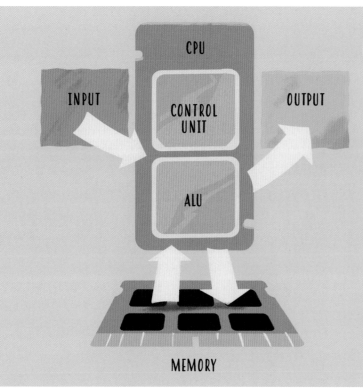

CPU PARTS

This diagram shows the basic parts of a CPU. The control unit (CU) directs the operation of the processor. It gets instructions and data from memory, as well as data from inputs to send to outputs. The arithmetic logic unit (ALU) performs calculations and logical operations, such as putting words into alphabetical order. The CPU also contains registers, which are bits of memory where instructions and data are stored while they are worked on.

INSTRUCTION CYCLE

Even though CPUs work at incredible speed, they can only follow one instruction at a time. For each instruction in a program, the CPU carries out a cycle of events called the fetch, decode, execute cycle. First, the CPU fetches the next program instruction from memory. Then, it decodes the instruction, so that it knows what data to get and what to do with the data. Finally, it executes the instruction. This happens millions of times every second.

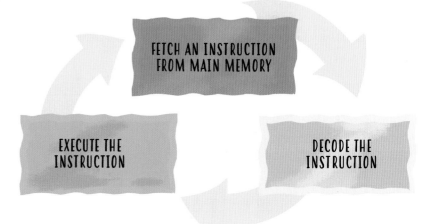

OUT OF CURIOSITY

Most modern CPUs have two or more cores. Each core is a like a mini processor inside the main processor. The cores work alongside each other, each doing its own calculations.

KEEPING COOL

Because of electrical **resistance**, all electric circuits warm up when electricity is flowing through them. The circuits inside a CPU produce quite a lot of heat, especially when the processor is working hard. A CPU can be damaged if it gets too warm, so the heat needs to be taken away. This is done with a fan that blows air over the processor. The CPU package has thin metal fins that provide plenty of surface area for the air to blow across.

GRAPHICS PROCESSING

Most personal computers have a graphics processing unit (GPU), as well as a CPU. The GPU takes the data about an image to be shown on-screen and turns it into a signal. It does all the complex calculations needed to produce smooth 3D graphics for games and other applications. This leaves the CPU free to perform other tasks. On desktop computers, the GPU is on its own circuit board, complete with cooling fans.

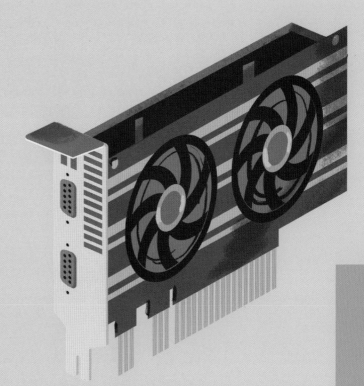

BINARY

Data is stored as binary numbers inside computers. The binary system uses only the digits 0 and 1. These digits, called bits, are easy to represent in electronic circuits by switching the current on or off, and the circuits can be used to perform operations such as adding and subtracting the binary numbers.

0 BINARY AND DECIMAL

2^7	2^6	2^5	2^4	2^3	2^2	2^1	2^0
128	64	32	16	8	4	2	1
1	1	0	0	0	1	0	0

This table shows how binary numbers compare to decimal numbers—the 0 to 9 system that we normally use. In **decimal**, the right-most place is units, then come tens, hundreds, and so on. In binary, the right-most is also units, but then come 2s, 4s, and so on, doubling each time. The binary number shown here represents 128 + 64 + 4 = 196 in decimal.

1 COUNTING IN BINARY

This table shows how the decimal numbers 0 to 15 are represented in binary using 4-digit binary numbers. The maximum decimal number that 4 binary digits can represent is 15—when all the digits are 1, the number is 8 + 4 + 2 + 1 = 15. Each time you add 1 in binary, the first digit changes from 0 to 1 or from 1 to 0. If it changes to zero, 1 is carried to the next column. Programmers often write numbers in hexadecimal, which is base 16.

Decimal	Binary	Hexadecimal
0	0000	0
1	0001	1
2	0010	2
3	0011	3
4	0100	4
5	0101	5
6	0110	6
7	0111	7
8	1000	8
9	1001	9
10	1010	A
11	1011	B
12	1100	C
13	1101	D
14	1110	E
15	1111	F

OUT OF CURIOSITY

Many computers work with numbers made up of 64 binary bits. A 64-bit number can represent integer numbers up to 18,446,744,073,709,551,615.

CIRCUIT OUTPUT = 1

CIRCUIT OUTPUT = 0

1 ON AND OFF

This example shows how binary numbers are represented in computer circuits. It's a simple circuit where closing a switch makes a light bulb glow, with the bulb representing a single binary digit. The number 1 is represented by closing the switch, making the bulb glow, and 0 is shown by opening the switch, making the bulb go out. Four of these circuits could be used to represent decimal numbers 0 to 15 in binary, as in the table on the opposite page.

0 BINARY LOGIC

Processors, memory chips, and other components contain circuits called **logic circuits**, which do simple operations on binary numbers. Working together, these circuits can do more complex operations such as adding and subtracting. NOT, OR, and AND gates are examples of logic gates. A logic table shows the result of each operation. For example, the output from an AND gate is only 1 when both inputs are 1.

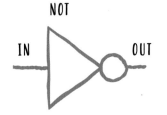

NOT

Input	Output
0	1
1	0

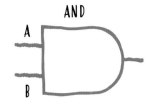

AND

Inputs		Output
A	B	
0	0	0
1	0	0
0	1	0
1	1	1

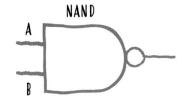

NAND

Inputs		Output
A	B	
0	0	1
1	0	1
0	1	1
1	1	0

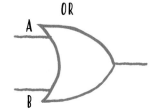

OR

Inputs		Output
A	B	
0	0	0
1	0	1
0	1	1
1	1	1

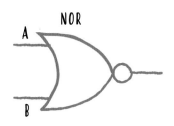

NOR

Inputs		Output
A	B	
0	0	1
1	0	0
0	1	0
1	1	0

MEMORY

Memory is where programs and data are stored inside a computer. The central processing unit is connected to the memory, so that it can get data from it and send data back. The simplest unit of memory is a bit. Each bit stores either a 0 or a 1. It has an address—a number that the processor uses to find it.

RANDOM ACCESS MEMORY

Random access memory (RAM for short) is the main type of memory in a computer. Each bit of information is stored by a tiny electric circuit, and there are millions of these circuits on a memory chip. Chips are connected to make up the memory the computer needs. In desktop computers, the chips are arranged on plug-in memory cards, so that more memory can be added. The processor can set each bit to 0 or 1 by sending a signal to its address and reading what data the bit holds. This is called writing and reading. The data in most types of RAM is lost when the power is switched off.

READ-ONLY MEMORY

Read-only memory (ROM) is memory that cannot have its contents changed by the processor. That means that it can only be read, not written to. ROM normally stores the programs and data that are needed when you first switch on a computer, when there are no programs and data in RAM. The data is put into ROM when the ROM is made, after which the data cannot be changed. Some types of ROM can be erased, then written again. For example, in EPROM (erasable programmable read-only memory), data can be erased by shining ultraviolet light on the chip before new data can be written to it.

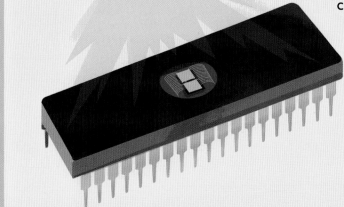

DATA ON THE BUS

The CPU is connected to the RAM chips and ROM chips by wires. Together, the wires are called a **data bus**. When the CPU reads memory, on or off signals from the memory travel along the bus to the CPU. When the CPU writes to memory, signals travel along the bus to the memory chips. An 8-bit bus (right) means eight bits of data travel along it at the same time, in parallel. Most modern PCs have 32-bit or 64-bit buses.

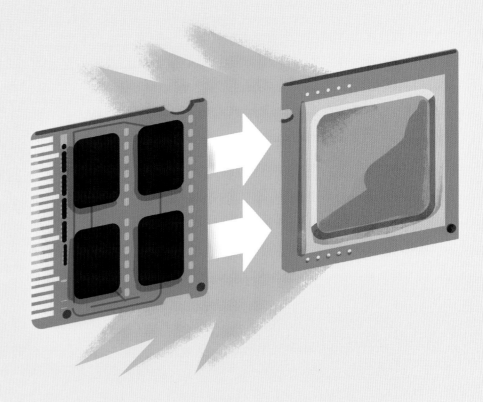

HOW MUCH MEMORY?

We are used to seeing the terms **megabyte** and **gigabyte** when talking about memory. These are the units used to measure the capacity of a memory chip and the amount of data in a file, such as a photo. The bit is the smallest unit of memory. It can store one binary digit (0 or 1). Next comes the byte, made up of 8 bits. This can store a decimal number from 0 to 255. The byte is used as the basic unit of memory.

bit (b)	single 0 or 1
byte (B)	8 bits
kilobyte (KB)	1024 bytes
megabyte (MB)	1024 kilobytes
gigabyte (GB)	1024 megabytes
terabyte (TB)	1024 gigabytes

STORAGE

The memory in a computer can only store a limited amount of data, and this is lost when the computer is switched off. That's why computers have storage where programs and data are kept. This storage does not lose its data when the power is off. Storage devices include hard disk drives, optical drives, and USB drives. They have a much greater storage capacity than the internal memory of computers.

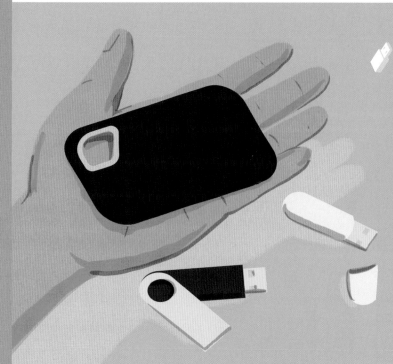

 INTERNAL AND EXTERNAL DRIVES

Most PCs have a large-capacity internal drive. This is either a hard disk drive (HDD) or a solid-state drive (SSD), perhaps 500 gigabytes or one terabyte in size. An HDD stores data on a spinning magnetic disk. An SSD stores data on memory chips. SSDs are faster and more reliable than HDDs. External drives are used to add extra storage or back up files. USB drives are small plug-in drives.

MEMORY CARDS

Small storage devices called **SD cards** are used to add additional storage to small devices such as smartphones and cameras. A memory card plugs into a device's card slot which contains electrical connections. Memory cards can be plugged into slots in computers or into USB card readers, so that data can be copied back and forth. There are two sizes of card: standard SD and microSD, with a range of storage capacities.

CLOUD STORAGE

When data is stored "in the cloud," it means that it is kept on a computer somewhere on the Internet, instead of being stored on a computer's internal or external drive. The advantage of cloud storage is that files can be accessed on any device, anywhere, as long as the device has an Internet connection. For example, a photo taken on a phone and stored in the cloud can be viewed on tablets and laptops. Cloud storage is cheaper than physical storage and is also good for backing up files.

ORGANIZING FILES

Files stored on a computer's drive or in the cloud can be programs, data that programs use, or data files, such as photos or documents. These files are stored in a logical file structure and given names so that they can be easily found. Files are organized inside folders. A file path shows the route through the file structure to find the file.

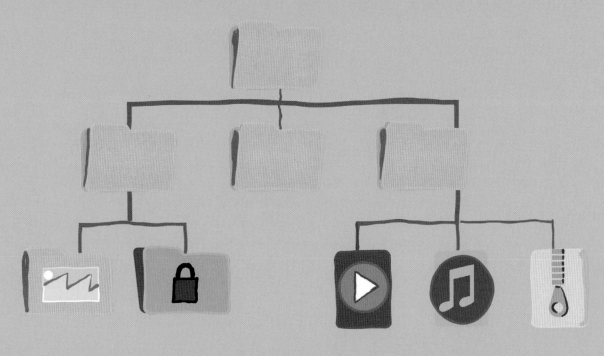

INPUTS

Computer systems get information from the outside world through inputs. Inputs include peripherals (devices) that you plug into USB ports, including external disk drives, and peripherals that connect with Bluetooth. Software (either the operating system or an application) takes information from the inputs when it needs it.

KEYBOARD, MOUSE, TRACKPAD

The most common inputs for a desktop computer or a laptop are a keyboard, a mouse, and a trackpad. A keyboard is used to input text and to control various functions of the computer. The mouse or trackpad are used to move the on-screen pointer (**cursor**) and select choices by clicking. On a tablet or smartphone, the touchscreen is an input that takes the place of the trackpad or mouse.

GAMES CONTROLLER

A games controller is another input device. It has one or two joysticks that detect both the direction and distance that the stick is moved, as well as many buttons. It can be wired or wireless. Games are designed to take inputs from a games controller for different actions. Specialist games controllers include flight sticks for flight simulators, and steering wheels and pedals for driving games. Some games controllers contain motion detectors.

TABLET

Designers and illustrators use drawing tablets to sketch, paint, and position objects on-screen. The device consists of a pad and a pen. The pad detects the position of the pen tip with great accuracy, and the pen detects how hard the tip is pressed on the pad and its angle. An **application** uses this information to control the size and angle of a paintbrush mark on the screen, for example. Some graphics pads allow drawing directly onto the screen, as though it were a sheet of paper.

ASSISTIVE TECHNOLOGY

Special input devices are made for people with disabilities. These are examples of assistive technology. A simple example is a Braille keyboard that allows people with impaired sight to use the keyboard. Other examples include head-tracking and eye-tracking devices that allow people to select objects on-screen by looking at them.

OUTPUTS

Computer systems send information to the outside world through outputs. Outputs include monitors, printers, and peripherals that you plug into USB ports, including external drives or ones that connect via Bluetooth. Software (either the operating system or an application) sends information to the outputs.

MONITORS

Monitors display images that are stored in the video memory of a computer. They are connected to a computer with a video cable, such as an HDMI cable. Signals are output to the monitor using the computer's graphics processing unit. The image on a monitor is made up of thousands of tiny dots called **pixels**. The screens on smartphones and tablets are also outputs. More powerful computers can output pictures to two or more monitors at the same time.

PRINTING

A printer is another example of an output device that provides physical copies of files stored on a computer. A printer can connect to a computer via a USB cable, Bluetooth, or over a local-area network. Software on the computer, called a printer driver, sends the data to the printer and controls how the printer puts ink on the paper.

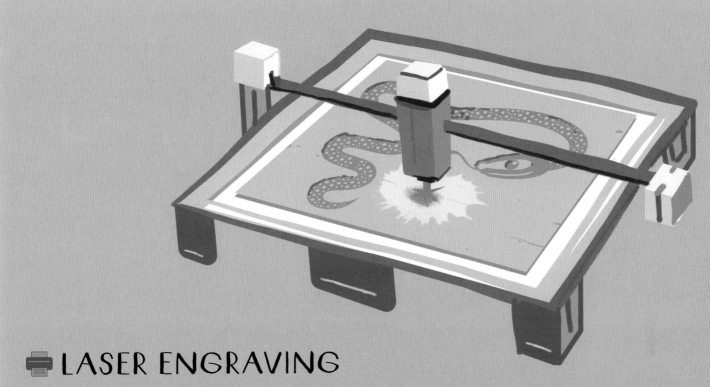

LASER ENGRAVING

A laser engraver is an output device that's a little bit like a printer. It features a low-power laser that cuts away material with a narrow beam. The laser is moved left, right, back, and forth (and sometimes up and down) by stepper motors. Laser-cutting software sends data to the laser cutter via USB or a network to a controller on the device. The controller directs the power, speed, and position of the laser beam to etch and cut materials, such as wood and acrylic.

WI-FI CONNECTIONS

Personal computers, tablets, smartphones, and many peripherals such as printers connect wirelessly to networks with Wi-Fi devices. These can be a built-in device or a plug-in Wi-Fi dongle. The Wi-Fi device acts as both an output and input for the computer. It sends data to the Internet through a Wi-Fi hub, or to other devices on a local area network. It also receives data from the Internet and other devices.

SOFTWARE

All the computer hardware that we have looked at so far in this chapter would be useless without software. Software is made up of programs and data. Programs tell a computer's processor what to do—how to process data and what to input and output. Software is made up of system software and application software.

⚙ OPERATING SYSTEMS

The operating system is software that controls the basic functions of a computer. It does jobs such as registering key presses from the keyboard or sending data to a printer. It's always working in the background on the computer. The operating system also works the user interface—moving the pointer, and opening and closing windows. The operating system is loaded into memory automatically when a computer is switched on. Microsoft Windows, Linux, Mac OS, and Android are all common operating systems.

SMARTPHONE SYSTEMS

Just like laptop and desktop computers, tablets and smartphones have operating systems. On a tablet or smartphone, the operating system runs the basic functions of a smartphone, such as the touchscreen, notifications, speakers, Wi-Fi, and Bluetooth. The two main operating systems for cellular (or mobile) devices are iOS (for Apple devices) and Android. The operating system software is stored in memory, which retains data even when the machine loses power.

ANTIVIRUS SOFTWARE

Malware is software than can damage the operating system, preventing the computer from working properly. Viruses are one type of malware. An operating system protects itself against malware by blocking other computers from connecting to a device over the Internet. Antivirus software can also be added to the operating system. This software keeps checking for viruses and removes them from the system.

KEEPING UP TO DATE

It's important to keep a computer's system software up to date. This makes sure that it works with new technology or software that the computer has. Downloading new systems software is known as a **system update**. New versions of the software also overwrite any bugs (mistakes) in the software. On personal computers, tablets, and smartphones, software updates normally happen automatically.

APPLICATIONS

An application is a piece of software that makes a computer do a certain job. System software stays the same and remains on the machine, but you choose which applications to run, depending on the job you want the computer to do. That might be browsing the Internet, word processing, or playing a game.

APP ICONS

The word "application" was originally used for the software that runs on desktop computers and laptop computers. The word "app" is short for application and is used mainly for software that runs on smartphones, tablets, and smartwatches. On these smart devices, apps have an icon that you tap in order to launch them. Several apps can be run at the same time.

EVERYDAY APPS

We use some apps every day to organize our lives, for messaging, email, checking calendars, and calculating. Some apps are for entertainment: music and video players, book and newspaper browsers, or photo viewers. There are also apps for web browsing and social media, or for changing settings on the machine—such as Wi-Fi signals or alert sounds.

OFFICE APPS

Apps designed for helping with office or schoolwork are run on most desktop and laptop machines. A collection of these apps is known as an **office suite**. The apps used most often are:

- A word processor for writing and editing documents
- A spreadsheet for recording data and doing calculations
- A presentation app for preparing slides for presentations
- A notebook app for taking and organizing notes

GAMES APPS

A games app turns a computer, tablet, or smartphone into a games machine. Games apps can be quite simple, such as puzzle games with 2D graphics, or complex, with detailed 3D graphics. A computer needs to be fast enough to run games with 3D graphics since these need plenty of processor power.

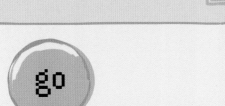

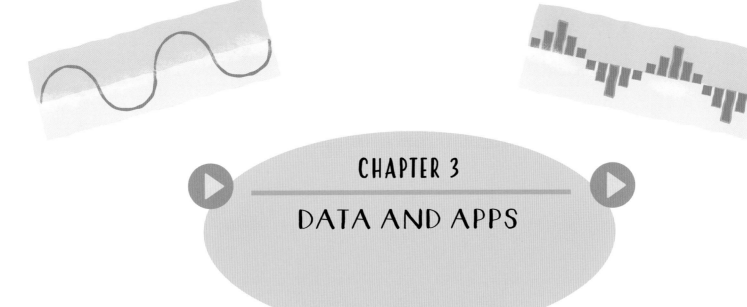

CHAPTER 3

DATA AND APPS

The job of a computer is to store and process data. The data can be numbers, text, images, video, or other information. All this data is represented in the computer as binary numbers, in the computer's memory, hard drives, memory sticks, or in the cloud. Applications (apps for short) are programs that make a computer do many different jobs, such as word processing, playing music, or gaming.

In this chapter, we look at how different kinds of data, such as text, photos, drawings, and sound, are stored as binary numbers. Then, we look at the main types of applications that are used to create and edit this data.

1 NUMBERS AND LETTERS

In our daily lives, we use decimal numbers in base 10, using the digits 0 to 9. Computers can only store and process binary numbers, so decimal numbers must be represented by binary numbers in a computer's memory. In text stored in a computer, letters are represented by binary numbers using simple codes.

1 BINARY AND DECIMAL

A single binary bit can only represent 0 or 1 in decimal. A byte (8 bits together) can represent decimal numbers up to 255. The more bits used to represent a number, the bigger the decimal number it can represent. Binary digits can be used to represent integers (whole numbers), negative numbers, and "floating point" numbers (numbers with digits after the decimal point). The table shows the size of whole numbers that different numbers of bytes can represent.

BINARY	DECIMAL
A BIT (0 OR 1)	0 OR 1
A BYTE (8 BITS)	0 TO 225
2 BYTES	0 TO 65,535
4 BYTES	0 TO 4,294,967,295

1 INPUTTING AND DISPLAYING NUMBERS

When using a computer or a device such as a calculator, we don't need to worry about binary. Although the numbers are stored in binary form, they are displayed in spreadsheets and calculators in decimal. The computer does the translation from binary to decimal for us. In the same way, when we enter a number on a calculator or keyboard, we type in decimal numbers, and the machine converts them to binary to be stored in the memory.

A LETTER CODES

Individual letters of the alphabet are represented in binary using a simple code made up of eight bits of information. The code is called **ASCII**, short for American Standard Code for Information Interchange. It was devised in the 1960s and has stayed the same ever since. The table below shows the binary and decimal numbers for each letter.

The code for capital letter A is 65. When a computer reads code 65 in text data, it always displays capital A. There are other ASCII codes for characters, such as a space (code 32) and a % sign (code 37).

Symbol	Decimal	Binary
A	65	01000001
B	66	01000010
C	67	01000011
D	68	01000100
E	69	01000101
F	70	01000110
G	71	01000111

There are now many more characters than the original 127 in the ASCII set. There are extra characters for letters and symbols in different alphabets from around the world. Two common codes are Unicode and UTF-8, which can represent thousands of characters, including **emojis**. A smiley face emoji has the Unicode code U+1F600.

CODE	BROWSER
U+1F600	
U+1F603	
U+1F604	
U+1F606	

OUT OF CURIOSITY

In 2022, there were 149,186 different characters in the Unicode character set. The characters include all the characters in 159 different scripts from around the world, including Chinese and Japanese characters.

IMAGE FILES

Photographs and other images, such as scans of text and drawings, are also stored as binary numbers in a smartphone, camera, or computer. The file for a photograph is made up by thousands of bits of binary data for the color of each dot in the photograph. There are different image file formats, such as JPEG or TIFF, organizing the data in a file in different ways.

PIXELS

A digital photograph or picture is made up of colored dots called pixels, arranged in a grid. This simple black-and-white smiley face is just 64 pixels in size. Each pixel is represented by a single bit of data (0 for white and 1 for black). Since there is a bit in the computer's memory or in a file for each pixel, the image is called a **bitmap** image.

COLOR DATA

In a color bitmap image, each pixel can be almost any color. In a typical camera image, the color of each pixel is represented by three bytes of data—one each for red, green, and blue. Each byte contains the level of brightness of each color, from 0 (no color) to 255 (full color). The different levels of red, green, and blue combine to make the pixel appear in its color. Using an image editor, the color of a pixel can be set by adjusting the levels of red, green, and blue with sliders.

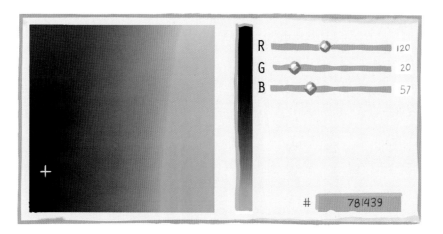

IMAGE FILE FORMATS

There are different types of image files, called file types or file formats. The file type is shown in the file extension, after the period in the name of the file, such as mydog.jpg. The most common image file formats are jpg, png, and tiff. In a digital camera, light falls on an image sensor when you take a photo, then software in the camera converts this into an image file.

DISPLAYING IMAGES

To display an image on the screen of a device, the device needs to know how to take the data from the file format that it's saved in. The device looks at the file extension to calculate how to read the file. At the start of the file, there is information about the size of the image, which the device uses to organize the data from the file to display the image.

VECTOR GRAPHICS

Computers store line drawings in a different way to the bitmap graphics used for photographs. The lines and shapes used in drawings are called vector graphics (a vector is a line that has certain length at a certain angle). In vector graphics, lines, curves, circles, and other shapes are represented by numbers. Vector graphics can show 2D drawings and 3D shapes.

BITAMP Vs VECTOR GRAPHICS

These two pictures show a line drawn as a bitmap and a **vector** graphic. The bitmap line has been drawn in a painting application, while the vector graphic was created using a vector-drawing application. The bitmap line is made up of pixels. The vector line is made up of an outline of points joined together with lines, then filled in to make it solid. The data for the outline is the position of the dots and how they are linked. The vector shape can be changed by moving the points on the line.

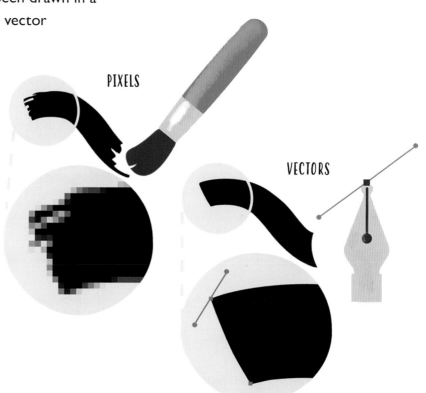

PIXELS

VECTORS

OUT OF CURIOSITY

The amazing, animated graphics we enjoy at the movies are known as computer-generated imagery (CGI). These graphics are very detailed 3D vector graphics drawn on computers using powerful graphics processors.

3D VECTORS

Three-dimensional objects can also be represented by vector graphics. The shapes are made up of points, lines between points, and flat surfaces between lines (called planes). The planes can be painted with shadings or bitmap patterns. A computer uses the data for the points, lines, and planes to draw a three-dimensional shape. Objects at the front of the picture hide objects behind them.

Three-dimensional vector graphics are used in games and computer-aided design (CAD). Objects that are going to be manufactured are designed using 3D drawing software, then the data is stored in files. The files can be sent to machines that make 3D objects. A 3D printer uses a 3D vector-graphics file to build an object using plastic.

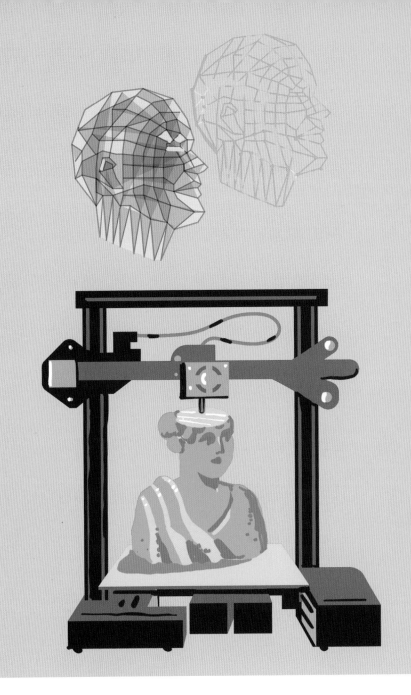

VECTOR MAPS

We can find our way around with digital maps, plan routes on personal computers, seek places to eat on smartphone maps, and follow directions using in-car GPS (global positioning), also called satellite navigation (satnav), systems. Digital maps are stored in a similar way to drawings. Road junctions are points on the ground that are linked by lines for roads. The software in navigation systems calculates routes between places using the map data.

VIDEO AND SOUND

We are used to watching videos and listening to music on our laptops and smartphones. As with text and images, video and sound are represented by binary data inside computers. Video and sound files can be very large.

RECORDING VIDEO ...

Many devices, including video cameras, smartphones, and laptops, can record video. Inside the camera is a light-sensitive chip that records an image of the scene the camera is pointed at. The camera turns the image into data for that frame. Then, it records another image. It repeats many times, typically 24 or 30 times a second, adding the data for each frame to the video file. Sound is recorded as part of the video file.

... AND VIEWING VIDEO

Video can be recorded in different formats. Common formats are MP4, ASI, and MOV. Computers, tablets, and smartphones have software that can read most video formats and display the videos on-screen. The device reads the file one image at a time and sends it to the screen. It repeats this process many times a second, so that we see a moving image.

🔊 SOUND RECORDING

Sound is made up of waves of air pressure. A microphone detects sound waves and outputs an electrical signal. The changing current in the signal represents the sound wave. This signal is an **analog** signal because its current can take any strength. It gets digitized and turned into a stream of binary numbers that represent the sound. Sounds can be stored in several formats, but the most common is the mp3 format.

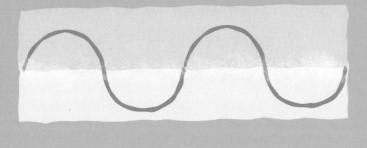

OUT OF CURIOSITY

Recording video uses up lots of memory because every second of video needs 20 or more images. So video is normally compressed. That means that if lots of pixels next to each other are the same shade, the shade and number of pixels is recorded, which takes up less data.

🔊 SOUND PROCESSING

Once a sound is recorded digitally, it can be played back as a file. This is how we listen to music on computers and other devices. Sound waves can be viewed on a screen to examine their shapes. Then they can be edited, cleaned up to get rid of unwanted noise, and cut-and-pasted together to make new sound waves. The pitch and volume of sounds can also be changed.

WORDS AND PICTURES

There are many apps for editing and organizing text, images, and other information on a page. A word-processing app allows editing of a text document. Desktop publishing apps are similar to word processing, but they have extra features for the design of posters, leaflets, and books. Presentation and web design software also allow you to edit and organize text, images, and video.

WORD-PROCESSING STAGES

When word processing, you start with a blank document. Then, you add text, graphics, images, and other elements. The word-processing document can be saved and edited as many times as needed before it's finally printed out or published online. Word processors help you with grammar and spelling, too.

Character	Paragraph

Lorem ip ▾ | 21 | A˅ a˅ | Aa |

- O Times New Roman
- O Trebuchet
- O **Arial Black**
- O ⊕⌘■♫♎⌘■♫♦
- O *Zapfino*

FONTS AND LAYOUT

A font is a collection of letters of the alphabet and other characters in a particular style. There are hundreds of different fonts to choose from on a word processor, using a drop-down menu. You can also change the font size, make text bold or italic, and change how the letters are spaced out. Text can be organized in headings and paragraphs, plus photos and diagrams can be added.

MAKING PRESENTATIONS

Presentation apps are used to display information to a group. This could be in a classroom, office, or training room. The presenter uses the app to build a series of slides. Each slide can include text, photos, diagrams, video, and sound. The slides are displayed one after the other on a screen or a projector. The person doing the presentation controls when one slide changes to the next.

WEB DESIGN

Websites all have text, graphics, images, video, sounds, and other features. Web design apps allow users to organize blocks of text, images, and so on, on to web pages. A web design app creates text code called HTML (HyperText Markup Language), as below. When you visit a website using a web-browsing app, the app decodes the HTML and displays the page for you.

```
<!DOCTYPE html>
    <html>
        <head>
            <title>Welcome to HTML</title>
        <head>
    <body>
        <h1> SIMPLE HTML CODE </h1>
        <p> HTML stands for Hyper Text Markup
Language </p>
        </body>
        </html>
```

SPREADSHEETS

A spreadsheet is an app for organizing and processing numbers. You can think of it as a complex calculator that does the work for you automatically. Accountants, engineers, and scientists make use of spreadsheets to help them with calculations.

ROWS AND COLUMNS

A spreadsheet file has rows (numbered from 1 at the top) and columns (alphabetically listed from A at the left), making a grid of cells. Each cell has a grid reference (the top left cell is A1). A cell can contain a number, or text, or a calculation formula. The most common spreadsheet app is Microsoft Excel, which has an .xlsx file extension.

	A	B	C	D	E
1	Student	English	Mathematics	Science	Total
2	Cindy	60	75	80	215
3	Nico	72	58	76	206
4	Eric	90	75	74	239
5	Leila	58	80	82	220

SPREADSHEET FORMULAS

A spreadsheet cell can contain a calculation formula, normally using data from other cells in the spreadsheet. In the spreadsheet above, the numbers in column E are calculated by adding the numbers in other columns in the same row. Cell E2 contains this formula. If you change the figures in the other columns, the figure in column E changes automatically.

$$=SUM(B2:D2)$$

EQUAL SIGN

FUNCTION NAME

ARGUMENT

SPREADSHEET CHARTS

A spreadsheet app can automatically draw charts using the data in its cells. These charts include line graphs, bar charts, and pie charts. Charts make it easier for somebody looking at the spreadsheet to understand what the data is showing. This bar chart describes the data in the spreadsheet.

ID No	NAME	DATE OF BIRTH	HEIGHT	WEIGHT
1	Bobby	01/04/68	72	170
2	Lilly	07/08/76	65	124
3	Carlos	06/11/93	68	130

DATABASES

A **database** is a collection of information that's organized in a logical way. A database is not the same as a spreadsheet because its data is not organized in cells in the same way as in a spreadsheet. Above is a simple database that records the date of birth, height, and weight for three people. A database application can ask questions about the data. For example, it could make a list of people over a certain height.

IMAGE EDITING

There are applications for creating and editing bitmap images and vector graphics. The most common use for image editing software is for editing photographs, perhaps to make them brighter or darker, to get rid of unwanted parts, or to remove imperfections.

 ADJUSTING PHOTOS

Designers often use an image-editing application together with a graphics tablet to edit photographs. The application has a range of tools for making changes to the image, such as a selection tool, paintbrushes, erasers, and tools for changing colors in the image. The graphics tablet has a drawing pen that senses how hard it is pressing onto the pad, providing the sensation of drawing naturally.

CROPPING AND SIZING

Cropping is chopping off parts of an image that are not needed. Cropping is normally done to make the interesting part of an image fill the whole picture, as with the seated reader to the right. Cropping is done by drawing a crop box and selecting the crop function. As well as being cropped, images can be resized so that they appear smaller or larger, and the resolution can be changed so that they take up less memory.

REMOVING STUFF

Image-editing software can be used to remove details from a photo. This might include objects in the background, such as a tree that appears above a person's head or even other people. Some image-editing software can do this automatically and fill in the space by duplicating other parts of the background.

VECTOR EDITING

A vector graphics editing application allows you to change the size, shape, color, angle, and fill pattern for vector graphics. Vector shapes have points joined by lines or curves. You can select and move a point to change the shape of the object and alter the angle of a curve where it joins a point. There are similar applications for editing 3D graphics.

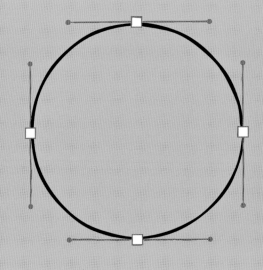

VIDEO AND AUDIO EDITING

Once video and audio have been recorded, they can be edited using a video- or audio-editing application. With these applications, an editor can cut out unwanted parts of video or sound, join sections together, and add special effects.

WORKING WITH FRAMES

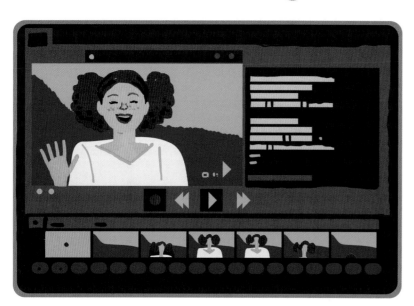

A video is made up of individual images called frames. When a video is played, the frames are played one after the other in quick succession. In a video-editing application, the frames appear on a timeline. Groups of frames called clips can be selected, moved around, or deleted, and the edited video played back. Titles and a soundtrack can be added to clips.

TRANSITIONS

A transition is a section of a video where one clip ends and another clip begins. Many different transition styles can be added in a video-editing application to make the video interesting and smooth to watch. They can control how the last few frames of one clip disappear and how the first few frames of the next appear. Examples of transitions are:
- A cut is a simple change from one clip to the next
- A fade makes the first clip slowly fade away as a new clip slowly fades in
- A wipe makes the first clip slide off screen and the next clip slide onto the screen

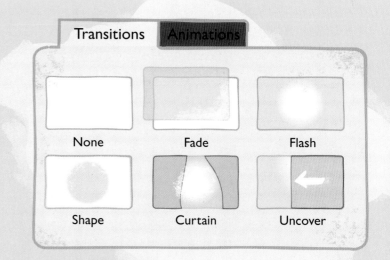

VISUAL EFFECTS

Video-editing software allows film editors to add visual effects (VFX) to their videos. They can lighten or darken areas of the video, change colors, or stretch or squash frames. Two videos can be mixed. One way of doing this is a technique called **green screen**. A person is filmed in front of a green background, and the video-editing software fills in the background with an image or another video.

AUDIO EDITING

A sound that's been recorded can be viewed on-screen as a sound wave. The sound can then be edited by chopping it up, moving parts around, and joining them together. Noises such as clicks and humming can be removed, too. Musicians, movie sound editors, and computer game producers are just some of the people who use audio-editing applications. There are apps that let you record and edit sound on a smartphone, too.

COLLECTING DATA

Every time you take a photograph on your smartphone, type a message into an email app, or search the Internet for a project, you are creating or collecting data.

DATA SURVEYS

If you conduct a survey, you are collecting data. You might do a survey about your friends' sports, hobbies, or pets, or gather information on traffic passing your school. You record the data by writing it down on a piece of paper or a tablet. Once you have the data, it can be entered into a spreadsheet to record it electronically. You can then display the data in charts and graphs.

ELECTRONIC DATA COLLECTING

Some data is collected and recorded automatically by machines. One example is a voting machine used during an election. Voters select the candidate they want to vote for by making a selection on a screen. The machine records the vote. Data from the machines is compiled to produce results. Other machines that collect data are cash registers and turnstiles at train stations.

SCIENTIFIC DATA

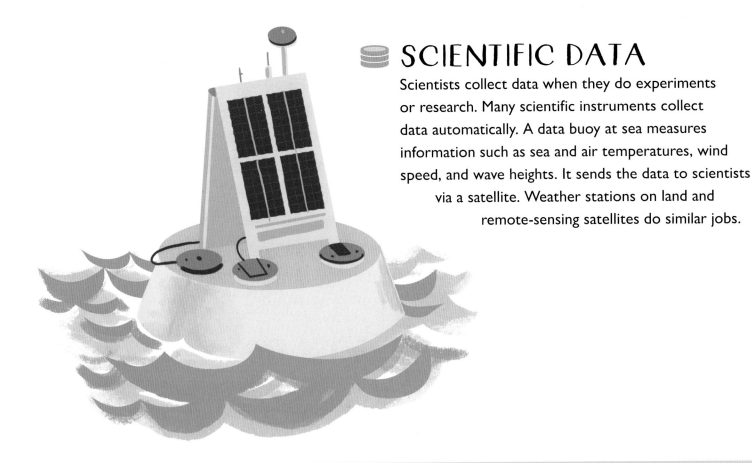

Scientists collect data when they do experiments or research. Many scientific instruments collect data automatically. A data buoy at sea measures information such as sea and air temperatures, wind speed, and wave heights. It sends the data to scientists via a satellite. Weather stations on land and remote-sensing satellites do similar jobs.

DATA FROM THE INTERNET

When you search the Internet for information on a subject, you are collecting data. You might copy and store this data on your computer. It's important to gather data from reliable websites. It's also important not to claim data from the Internet, such as documents and photographs, as your own.

http://search

Search

SCRATCH

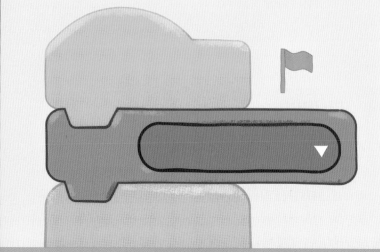

python

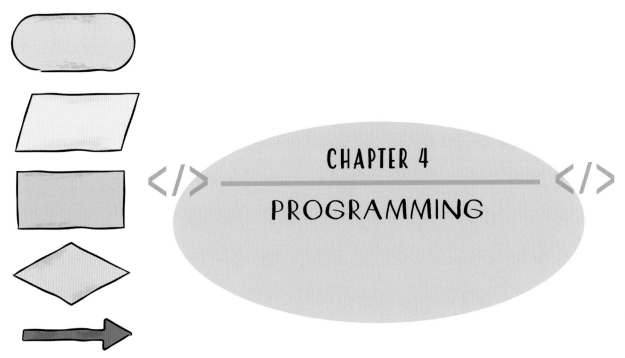

CHAPTER 4

PROGRAMMING

A program is a series of instructions for the computer. Different programs make a computer do different tasks, such as word processing or playing music. Writing computer programs (called coding) is the job of computer programmers. A programmer needs a logical mind and mathematical skills.

This chapter look at how programmers break down problems into simple steps before they start coding, often using flow diagrams. It looks at different types of data, how programs can change data and make decisions, plus different programming languages.

THINKING LIKE A PROGRAMMER

Programmers need to be very logical. A program might
have thousands of instructions, and these need to be
carefully organized or the program might not work properly.
Programmers use computational thinking, which means that
they design programs in a logical way.

BREAKING DOWN A PROBLEM

Before programmers start writing the code for a new program, they look at
what the program needs to do. The problem gets broken down into simple
steps, then the code for each step is figured out. The stages include:

DECOMPOSITION • Breaking a problem into smaller problems
and breaking a programming project
into small chunks

ABSTRACTION • Concentrating on the jobs that the program
needs to do and ignoring what's not necessary

ALGORITHMS • Finding out how the program is going to do each job
it needs to do, then writing the code for each step

CODING

Programmers write programs in a language that a computer
can understand. This is called programming, or coding.
Programmers write code on-screen using editing programs to
help them. They often work in teams, breaking up coding into
sections for each programmer. Programs are always tested
before they are used. Any problems (called bugs) are ironed
out. This process is called debugging.

FLOW DIAGRAMS

A programmer might draw a picture called a step-by-step flow diagram to show how an operation, or algorithm, works. A flow diagram is made up of boxes connected by arrows. Each box contains a step in the algorithm. The diagram helps a programmer figure out the logical flow of the program before writing any code.

➡ FLOW CHART SHAPES

You'll find different-shaped boxes in a flow chart.
Each shape has a different type of instruction inside.

Start/End

A BOX WITH ROUNDED ENDS SHOWS WHERE A PROGRAM BEGINS OR ENDS.

Input/Output

A SLOPED BOX SHOWS INSTRUCTIONS THAT RECEIVE OR OUTPUT DATA (SUCH AS GETTING A KEY PRESS FROM A KEYBOARD OR PRINTING A NUMBER ON-SCREEN).

Process

A RECTANGULAR SHAPE IS A PROCESS BOX. IT SHOWS INSTRUCTIONS TO BE PERFORMED, SUCH AS NUMBER ADDITION.

Decision

A DIAMOND SHOWS AN INSTRUCTION THAT MAKES A DECISION, SUCH AS WHETHER A NUMBER IS POSITIVE OR NEGATIVE.

ARROWS SHOW THE FLOW OF THE PROGRAM BETWEEN BOXES.

Arrows

A QUIZ GAME FLOW CHART

Here is a flow chart for a simple computer quiz that uses all the different box shapes. In the game, each time the user gets a question right, they can decide to proceed and answer another question. The prize money is doubled for each correct answer.

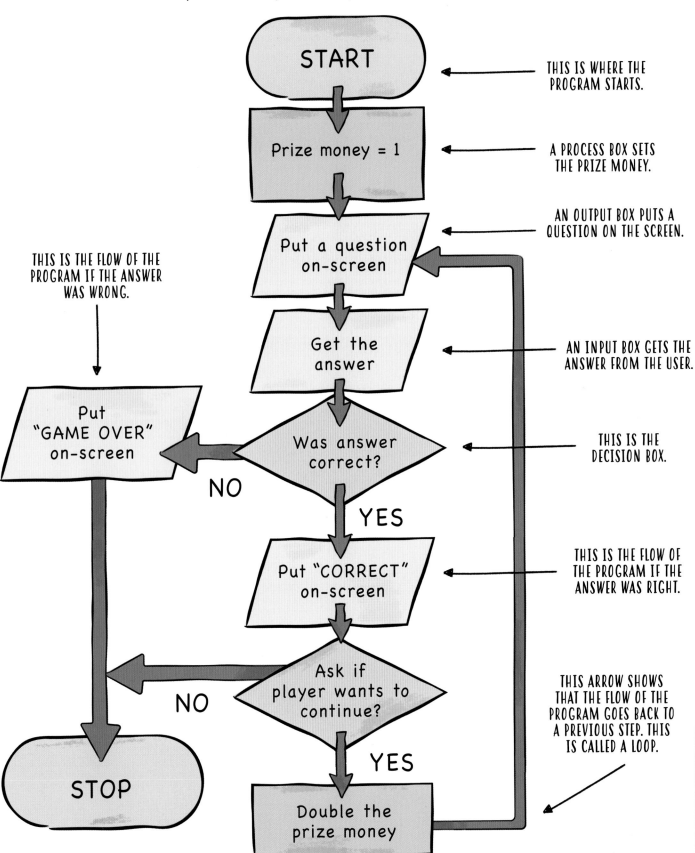

THIS IS WHERE THE PROGRAM STARTS.

A PROCESS BOX SETS THE PRIZE MONEY.

AN OUTPUT BOX PUTS A QUESTION ON THE SCREEN.

THIS IS THE FLOW OF THE PROGRAM IF THE ANSWER WAS WRONG.

AN INPUT BOX GETS THE ANSWER FROM THE USER.

THIS IS THE DECISION BOX.

THIS IS THE FLOW OF THE PROGRAM IF THE ANSWER WAS RIGHT.

THIS ARROW SHOWS THAT THE FLOW OF THE PROGRAM GOES BACK TO A PREVIOUS STEP. THIS IS CALLED A LOOP.

START

Prize money = 1

Put a question on-screen

Get the answer

Was answer correct?

Put "GAME OVER" on-screen

NO

YES

Put "CORRECT" on-screen

Ask if player wants to continue?

NO

STOP

YES

Double the prize money

TYPES OF DATA

Programmers use different types of data to store and process information. In a game program, the score would be stored as number data and the name of the player as a series of characters, or string data. Programmers need to use the correct type of data to make a program work properly.

CHARACTERS

A character is a single letter, digit, or symbol. It's stored in memory as a number in ASCII code or another type of code. For example, the capital letter A is stored as 65. When you type a letter on a keyboard, the key press is stored as a character.

STRINGS

A string is a made up of characters. There can be thousands of characters in a string or no characters at all (when the string is described as an empty string). A password is an example of a string—it's a list of letters and other characters. Strings can be joined together or taken apart. When you type in a password, a new character is added to the string each time.

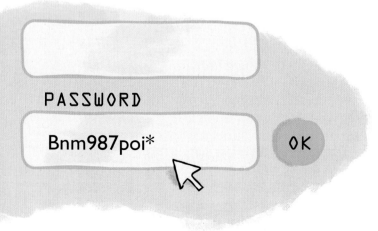

PASSWORD

Bnm987poi*

OK

INTEGERS

An integer is a whole number, such as 5 or 135, with no digits after the decimal point. An integer can be positive or negative. In a program, an integer is used for jobs such as keeping a score in a basketball game, which is always a whole number. Integers are also used for counting how many times a program has been around a loop.

REAL NUMBERS

A real number is one that can have any value. It can have digits after the decimal point and also be negative or positive. In programming, a real number can be used to store very large or very small numbers. In a computerized timing system for athletics, the finishing time for a race is recorded as a real number.

BOOLEANS

Computer programs often use logic. Boolean data records whether something is true or false. A program might test to find out if a number is positive. If it is, then the result would be true, otherwise the result would be false.

OUT OF CURIOSITY

Boolean data is named after British mathematician George Boole, who lived in the nineteeth century. Boole developed the true-or-false system of logic.

(x) VARIABLES (x)

In a computer program, variables are used to store data that needs to be remembered while the program is running. A variable always has a name that the program uses to find it or change its value. A programmer might use a variable called "yearborn" to store the year that someone is born, for example. There are different types of variables for the different types of data that a computer can store and process.

(x) NAMING VARIABLES

A variable is given a name and a value using an equals sign, which is called the **assignment operator**. The first two statements below name variables A and B and give them values of 10 and 20.
A and B are integer variables.
The statement A = B changes the value of A from 10 to 20. The statements, to the right, name two string variables and give them values.

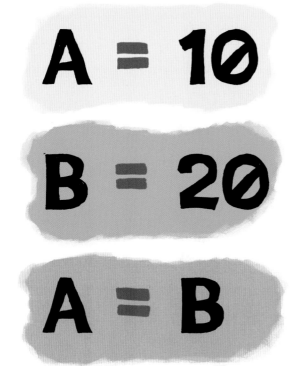

(x) ARRAYS

An array is like a table of data with a variable name, with numbered pigeonholes called **elements**.
Each element can store a different value. Here, the array called runner_name has three elements. A value can be assigned like this: runner_name (2) = "Harry"

name = "Joe"

password = "woofwoof2"

runner_name (1)
runner_name (2)
runner_name (3)

(x) INPUTTING VARIABLES

Often, a program needs to get data from the person using the program. This is done using an input statement. The user types the value of a variable into a box and presses the ENTER key, or they select a value by swiping bars on a touchscreen. The program then sets variables to the values that the user typed in. Such inputs might be found on a shopping website.

First name

Last name

Address

Submit

(x) OUTPUTTING VARIABLES

A program may also need to show what the value of a variable is. It does this with an output statement. A print statement is an output statement that prints the value of a variable on the screen or to a printer. Here, the print statements send the values of variables called "name" and "A" to the screen.

PRINT (name)   Joe

PRINT (A)   20

✳ OPERATORS

Operators are symbols that make a computer do arithmetic, compare two things, or make logical calculations. In a program, they are used for calculations and making decisions. Some operators also work on strings.

✳ ARITHMETIC OPERATORS

There are arithmetic operators for adding, subtracting, multiplying, dividing, and for the calculation of powers of numbers, such as squares. Here are some examples:

A = B + 1
means make variable A equal to variable B plus 1

A = B − 2
means make variable A equal to variable B minus 2

A = B * 3
means make variable A equal to variable B multiplied by 3

A = B / 4
means make variable A equal to variable B divided by 4

A = B ^ 2
means make variable A equal to variable B squared

The plus operator also works with strings. Adding two strings joins them to make one long **string**. There are other operators for chopping strings into pieces, too.

✳ CALCULATING IN ORDER

Arithmetic operators can be combined to do more complicated calculations in a single statement. For example, the statement A = B * 2 + 5 means multiply B by 2 then add 5, then make A equal to the answer. If B was equal to 2, A would become equal to 9.

The program does the operators in order—powers first, then division, multiplication, addition, then subtraction. Parentheses (brackets) make part of a statement happen first.

Here, the parentheses mean that D is divided by four first. Then C is multiplied by 2. Then, these two results are added to B. A is made equal to the answer.

✳ BIGGER OR SMALLER?

Comparison operators compare the values of numbers or variables. They are used in statements called IF–THEN statements to decide which statements the program will execute next.

THE DOUBLE EQUAL SIGN (==) MEANS "IS EQUAL TO." A STATEMENT SUCH AS "IF A == 5 THEN B = 10" WOULD TEST TO SEE IF VARIABLE A WAS EQUAL TO 5, AND IF IT WAS, IT WOULD MAKE B EQUAL TO 10.

> THE › SIGN MEANS GREATER THAN.

< THE ‹ SIGN MEANS LESS THAN.

✳ LOGICAL OPERATORS

Logical operators work on **Boolean data** (data that can only have the value TRUE or FALSE). They are also called Boolean operators and are used to combine results found using comparison operators.

The AND operator gives a TRUE answer if both statements are TRUE. For example:

IF first_name = "Bob" AND second_name = "Smith" THEN PRINT "Your name is Bob Smith."

The OR operator gives a TRUE answer if one or the other statement is TRUE. For example:

IF first_name = "Bob" OR first_name = "Sue" THEN PRINT "You are Bob or Sue."

OUT OF CURIOSITY

The results of logical operations such as AND, OR, and NOT are shown in tables called truth tables.

AND
OR
NOT

A program is made up of instructions that a computer follows. It starts from the first instruction, then follows other instructions in turn. This is called program flow. Usually, there are branches where program flow goes one way or another, and loops where program flow goes back and repeats instructions.

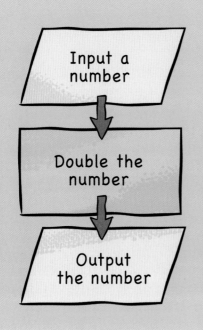

A SIMPLE SEQUENCE

Most of the time, the flow of a program moves from one instruction to the next. Each instruction is completed, then the next carried out. This simple program doubles a number. It has three instructions, and the flow goes from the top to the bottom.

BRANCHING

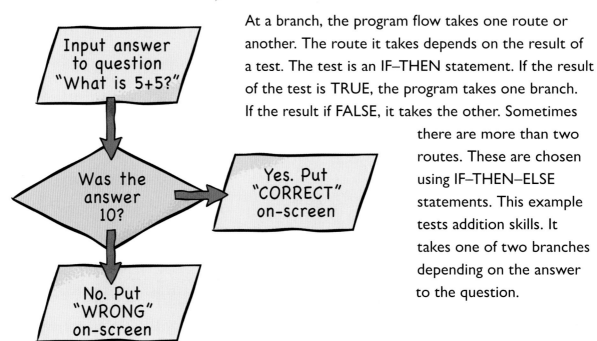

At a branch, the program flow takes one route or another. The route it takes depends on the result of a test. The test is an IF–THEN statement. If the result of the test is TRUE, the program takes one branch. If the result if FALSE, it takes the other. Sometimes there are more than two routes. These are chosen using IF–THEN–ELSE statements. This example tests addition skills. It takes one of two branches depending on the answer to the question.

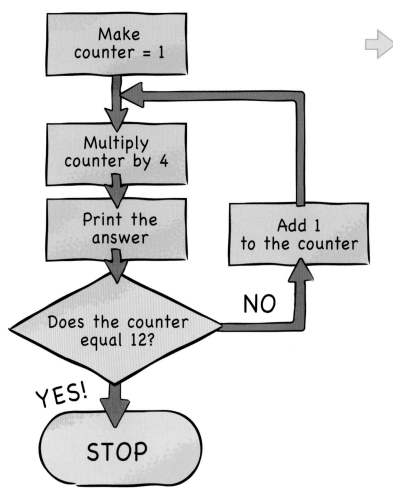

Programs often repeat the same instructions. Instead of writing the same instructions many times over, programmers put these instructions in a structure called a loop. The program flow goes around and around the loop until the process that the loop is doing is completed.

This program prints the four-times table—4, 8, 12, and so on, until 48. The counter starts at 1. The program flow goes back to the start of the loop, adding 1 to the counter each time, until the counter reaches 12.

⇨ SUBROUTINES

Programmers sometimes need to use the same set of instructions at different points in a program. Instead of repeating the instruction at each point, they write the instructions once in a mini program called a **subroutine**. Each time the instructions are needed, the program flow goes to the subroutine. At the end of the subroutine, the flow returns to the main program. In this example, the subroutine prints a name.

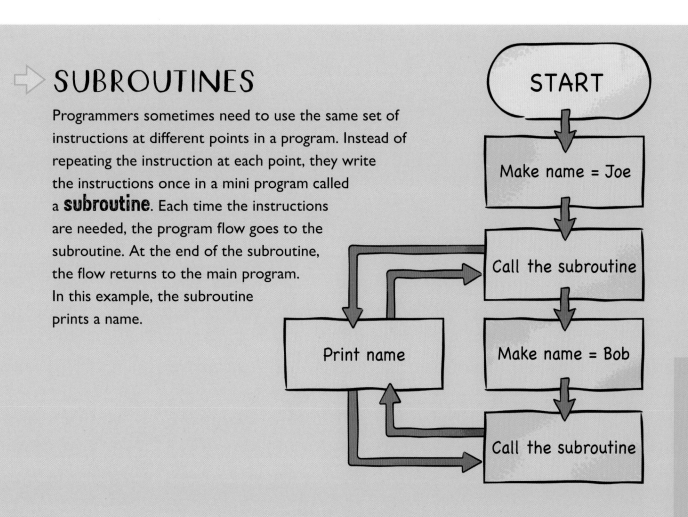

</> LANGUAGES </>

Programmers write programs using programming languages. Examples are Python, Scratch, Java, and C++. The computer translates the programming language into machine code that its processor can understand.

</> EXAMPLE LANGUAGES

There are dozens of different languages. Each one is designed for programmers to do different jobs, such as creating interactive websites or writing games. Here are some common examples.

Scratch is a simple language designed for beginners learning programming. It's called a block programming language.

Python is used to program software for websites and apps. It's a good first programming language to learn.

JavaScript is often used to write interactive content on websites. It's a scripting language, which means that the computer reads the program one line at a time. It turns each line into machine language and executes it.

C++ is a more advanced programming language used for writing complex games, operating systems, and apps.

OUT OF CURIOSITY

C++ is an example of a "compiled" language. This means that the whole program is turned into machine language before it's executed.

BLOCK PROGRAMMING

Many children write their first computer program with a block programming language such as Scratch. A program is built up by dragging and dropping blocks to link them together. There are different blocks for different types of instructions. It's easy to see the flow of the program and if it is working properly since the results appear on-screen.

</> SCRIPT PROGRAMS

A program written in a scripting language, such as Python or JavaScript, looks like a list of instructions. In each instruction, there might be variable names, operators, and commands. A command tells the computer to do something specific, such as input or print a variable. This simple Python program defines two strings, joins them to make a new string, and prints that string out.

```
string1 = "pyt"
string2 = "hon"
joined_string = string1
+string2
print(joined_string)
```

BUGS AND DEBUGGING

Programmers always test the programs they write to make sure they do the job they are supposed to do. Programs often don't work the first time they are tested because they contain mistakes called bugs. The computer might say that the program contains a **syntax error**, which means an instruction doesn't follow the rules of the programming language. Putting the errors right is called debugging.

Syntax error

BLOCK PROGRAMS

Programming using blocks is drag-and-drop programming or visual programming, because it's easy to see the structure and flow of the program.
Block programming is a great introduction to programming.

In a block programming language such as Scratch, different blocks of the code appear in different shades. This makes it easy to build instructions and see how the program works. Here are some examples.

Yellow blocks are "event" blocks—the program uses them to detect when things happen.

Blue blocks are "motion" blocks—they are used to control the movement of **sprites** on the screen.

Orange blocks are "control" blocks—they control the flow of a program.

Green blocks are "operator" blocks—they contain different operators such as adding and subtracting.

Dark orange blocks are "variables" boxes—they are used to set and change variables.

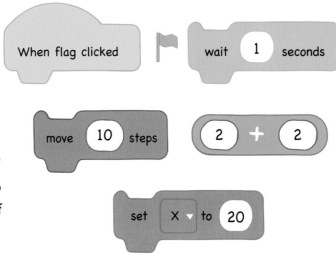

When flag clicked

wait 1 seconds

move 10 steps

2 + 2

set X to 20

SIMPLE FLOW

This simple program has just four instructions. The first block is an event block. When the green flag on-screen is clicked, it starts the program. The second block sets the variable called time to the value 2. The third block makes the character on-screen say "Hello" for the number of seconds contained in the variable time. The final instruction stops the program.

When flag clicked

Set time to 2

say Hello! for time seconds

stop all

Hello!

BLOCK LOOPS

This block program makes the character say the four times table up to 40. It does this using a repeat loop. The "repeat 10" instruction means that the two instructions inside the loop are repeated ten times. Each time, the counter increases by one. After ten repeats of the loop, the stop statement ends the program.

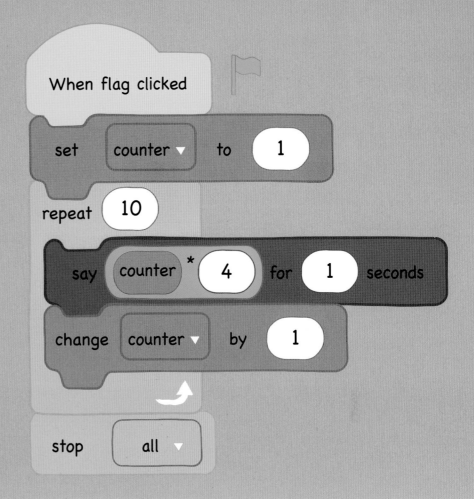

When flag clicked

set counter to 1

repeat 10

say counter * 4 for 1 seconds

change counter by 1

stop all

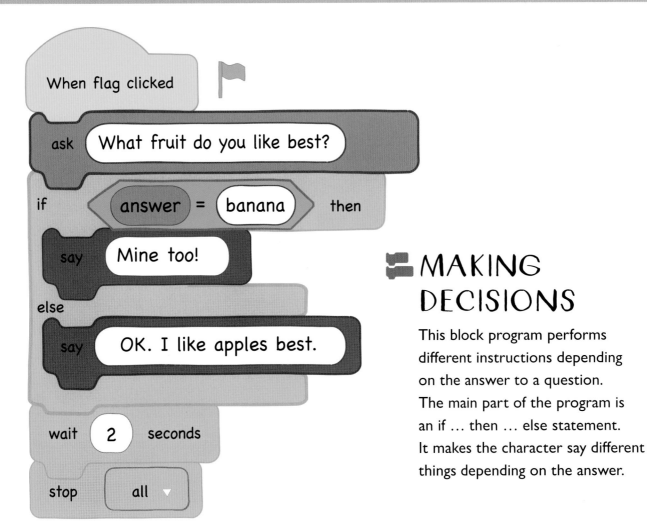

When flag clicked

ask What fruit do you like best?

if answer = banana then

say Mine too!

else

say OK. I like apples best.

wait 2 seconds

stop all

MAKING DECISIONS

This block program performs different instructions depending on the answer to a question. The main part of the program is an if ... then ... else statement. It makes the character say different things depending on the answer.

SCRIPT PROGRAMS

Here are some simple programs written in Python. They are examples of programming with scripts. The statements look like the words in block programming, but the programmer must write them in a text editor. They are executed by the computer one at a time.

</> SIMPLE SCRIPTS

This simple program contains a series of statements. The first two lines name the variables a and b, and give them values of 10 and 20. The third line prints the sum of a and b. The fourth and fifth lines print a × b. The final two lines name the variable name and print it out. In this simple script, it's quite easy to understand what's going on.

```
a = 10
b = 20
print (a + b)
c = a * b
print (c)
name = "Bob"
print (name)


>>>
30
200
Bob
```

OUT OF CURIOSITY

The Python programming language was developed by Dutch programmer Guido van Rossum in the early 1990s. Van Rossum named it after the British comedy show *Monty Python's Flying Circus*.

SCRIPT LOOPS

Here's a simple loop written in the Python scripting language that prints some of the four times table. The first statement tells the computer to execute a loop. It uses a variable called "i" to count the number of times it does the loop, and the (10) tells it to complete the loop 10 times. The variable "i" automatically goes up by one each time the loop is completed. The indent (space at the beginning) on the second line shows that this statement is part of the loop. It uses the print command to print i times 4, and puts a comma and space after it. In Python, the loop begins with i equal to zero and ends with i equal to 9, not 1 and 10 as you might expect.

```
for i in range (10)
    print (i*4, end=', ')


0, 4, 8, 12, 16, 20, 24, 28, 32, 36,
```

BRANCHING PYTHON

Here's an example of branching using Python. It's like the earlier block programming program but written in script instead. The first line uses the input command. The command prints the question on-screen, waits for a reply to be typed in, then makes the string variable answer equal to the reply. Line 2 tells the computer what to do if the answer was "banana." In this case, it completes any indented instructions. The "else'"command tells the computer what to do if the answer was anything other than "banana."

```
answer = input ("What's your favorite fruit?")
if answer == "banana":
    print ("Mine too!")
else:
    print ("OK. The apple is my favorite.")
```

CHAPTER 5

COMPUTER COMMUNICATIONS

Computers are nearly always connected to other computers or peripherals, such as printers and hard drives. Data travels along the connections from one machine to another, so that the machines can communicate. Connections can be between machines in the same room or on different sides of the world.

This chapter looks at connections with wires and without wires (wireless). It looks at how data travels along these connections and how computers are connected to make networks—including the Internet. Finally, it looks at the dangers of connecting devices to networks.

SIMPLE CONNECTIONS

You can connect a computer to a nearby device, such as a printer, a smartphone, an external storage drive, or a pair of headphones, with a cable or wireless radio connection.

USB CONNECTIONS

The letters **USB** are short for Universal Serial Bus. USB is the most common way of connecting computers and other devices to each other with cables. The word "serial" means that the data travels along a single wire. There are several kinds of USB connectors. Each one can be used for charging as well as exchanging data. A USB hub plugs into a computer to give you several sockets for USB plugs or data cards.

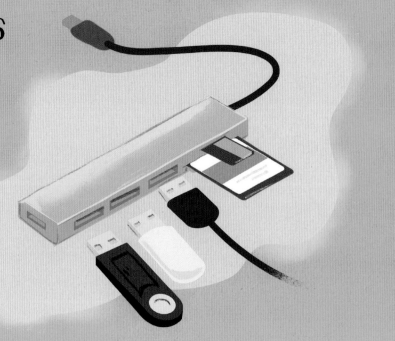

BLUETOOTH

Wireless connections are often used to connect laptop computers and smartphones to earbuds, headphones, and speakers. The most common wireless communication system is called **Bluetooth**. This uses radio waves to send data over short distances. Devices need to be "paired" before they can exchange data to make sure that the data is going to the right place.

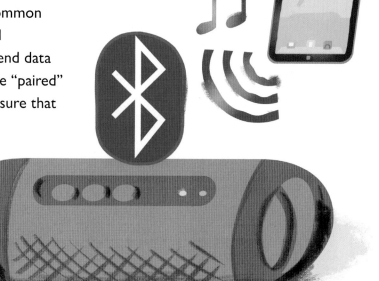

OUT OF CURIOSITY

The inventors of Bluetooth named it after King Harald Bluetooth, who ruled Denmark more than a thousand years ago. It is said that he had a dead tooth that was blue. The name chosen for the tech was supposed to be temporary, but it stuck.

SERIAL SIGNALS

Both USB and Bluetooth are serial systems, which means that the data travels one bit at a time along a cable or as a radio signal. An electronic system called a serial interface breaks up the data into single bits and sends it one bit after the other. At the receiving end, another serial interface rebuilds the data. In a cable, a serial signal is made by switching the current on and off to represent the binary bits (on for 1s and off for 0s).

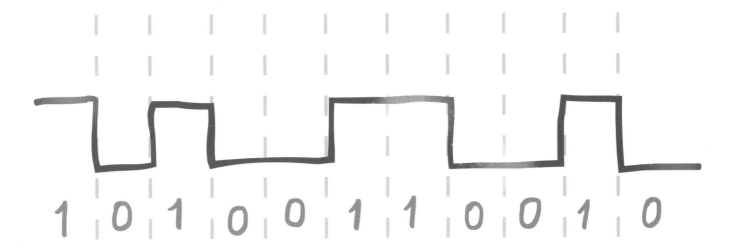

DATA SPEEDS

The faster that data gets from one device to another—the transfer rate—the better. Faster connections mean that we wait less time for data to arrive. Transfer rates are measured by how many bits travel along a wire or by radio signal every second. A megabit per second (Mbps) means a million bits per second, and a gigabit per second (Gbps) means a billion bits per second. A typical USB speed is 480 Mbps, and the fastest Bluetooth speed is about 25 Mbps.

NETWORKS

Two or more computers or devices are often connected to each other so they can share and exchange data. The arrangement is called a computer network. Networks can be just two computers in the same room. The Internet, which links millions of computers around the world, is also a network.

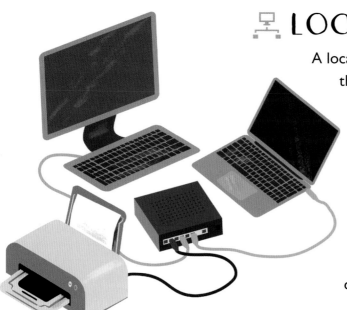

LOCAL AREA NETWORKS

A local area network (LAN for short) is a network that links computers and other devices near each other. A network of devices in the same room, house, or office is a local area network. The devices on a local area network can exchange data with each other. Here is a wired local area network that connects a desktop computer, laptop computer, and a smart television. Each device is connected to a switch that controls the flow of data between the devices.

WIDE AREA NETWORKS

A wide area network (WAN) is a network that covers a greater area than a local area network. It might link computers and devices on many different floors of a building, in separate buildings, or different sites for an organization around a country. A WAN is usually made up of local area networks linked to each other. The Internet is a vast WAN that covers most the world.

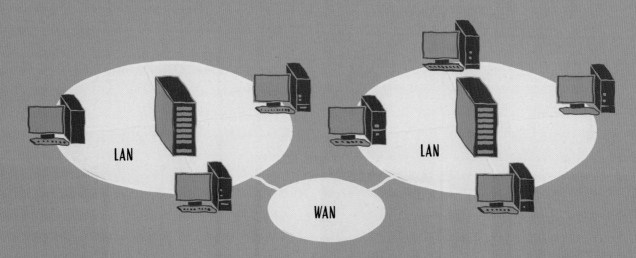

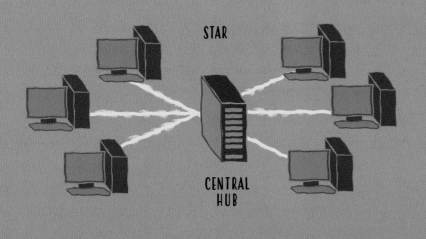

STAR

CENTRAL
HUB

RING

NETWORK SHAPES

The computers and other devices on a local area network
or a wide area network can be connected in different
ways. These are called network topologies. The shape used
might depend on where each machine is, or on how easy
it is to install cables. Some shapes are not very practical.
For example, in a ring network, all the machines must be
switched on for the network to work.

BUS

NETWORK
BACKBONE

ETHERNET LINKS

The machines on wired local area
networks are linked together by
standard ethernet cables. An
ethernet cable has a plug on
each end that plugs into
a port on each machine,
and each machine has an
ethernet interface that
sends and receives signals.
This network switch has
several ports. Each machine
on the network has an ethernet
address, so that data can find its
way to the right place.

WIRELESS NETWORKS

In a local area network, the links between the computers and other devices are often wireless, which means that the data travels by radio signals instead of through cables. A wireless network is also called a Wi-Fi network. Wireless networks are convenient for cellular (mobile) devices.

A HOME WI-FI NETWORK

You might have a wireless network at home. The main reason for having a home network is to link devices to the Internet, although the devices can exchange data over the network, too. Most wireless networks have a box called a **router** that sends and receives data for devices. Each device has an address to make sure that the data goes to the right place.

PROS AND CONS

A Wi-Fi network is easy to set up because it doesn't need any cables going around walls and under floors. Its main disadvantage is that the signals sometimes can't get through obstructions, so boosters are needed. Many home and office networks use a mixture of wires and wireless connections.

WI-FI HUB

Most home Wi-Fi networks are linked to the Internet, so that devices on the network can be used for web browsing, sending emails, gaming, and using social media apps. A box called a modem router, or "Wi-Fi hub", does two jobs. The modem section sends and receives data to and from the Internet, while the router is part of the local Wi-Fi network.

OUT OF CURIOSITY

The term "Wi-Fi" isn't short for anything. It came from "hi-fi," which stands for high fidelity, meaning very high-quality sound recording and playback.

SMARTPHONE INTERNET

The radio signals on a Wi-Fi network are quite weak, so in some places, especially outdoors, there is no signal. Instead, smartphones and tablets link to the Internet using data signals from a cellular (mobile) network, provided they are in range of a network aerial. Transfer speeds improve with every generation of cellular (mobile) network, the latest being the fifth generation—5G for short.

THE INTERNET

The Internet is vital for modern communications. We use it for getting information, shopping, booking vacations, banking, and hundreds of other jobs. The Internet is a network of networks. It connects millions of computers and other devices across the world.

INTERNET STRUCTURE

The Internet can link a smartphone to a laptop on the other side of the world. Data can move between the two machines almost instantly. You can make a video call to a relative living on another continent, with live video data moving both ways.

The Internet is made up of thousands of networks linked together by the Internet backbone. The backbone is like a super high-capacity freeway for data. It's made of optical cables that move data around the world as light signals at almost the speed of light. At the junctions on the backbone are superfast routers that make sure data gets to the right place.

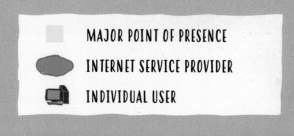

MAJOR POINT OF PRESENCE
INTERNET SERVICE PROVIDER
INDIVIDUAL USER

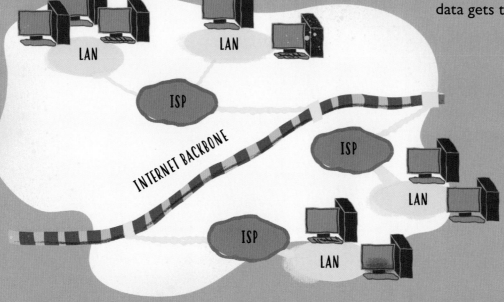

Most computers and other devices connect to the Internet through an organization called an Internet Service Provider (ISP). ISPs provide access to the Internet. When you are browsing the Internet, data comes from the Internet backbone through the computers of an ISP, then along a cable to your home.

SERVERS

A server is a computer connected to the Internet where information is stored that we can access online. Servers store websites, emails, databases, photographs, and other data that we store in the "cloud." When a computer needs information, such as a web page, it sends a request through the Internet to a server, and the server sends the information back.

DATA CENTERS

A data center is a place where a large amount of data is stored on servers. When you visit the website of a large organization, the data you get will probably come from a data center. That might be posts from a social media app or a list of games available on a shopping website.

BACKBONE CONNECTIONS

The backbone of the Internet carries vast amounts of data between major cities, countries, and continents. Many backbone cables are underwater, resting on the seabed, crossing oceans, or following coasts. It's easier to lay them on the seabed than to bury them underground.

HOW THE INTERNET WORKS

Vast amounts of data is hurtling around the Internet all the time. So how does all that data find its way to the right computer or smartphone? The answer is that every device that's on a network connected to the Internet has its own unique internet address.

PACKETS OF DATA

Imagine downloading an image from a website on the Internet. The image file does not travel from the server where it's stored to your computer in one big lump. Instead, it's broken up into small chunks called packets. Each packet travels separately, and packets might take different routes through the Internet. When they arrive, the packets are reassembled into the original file.

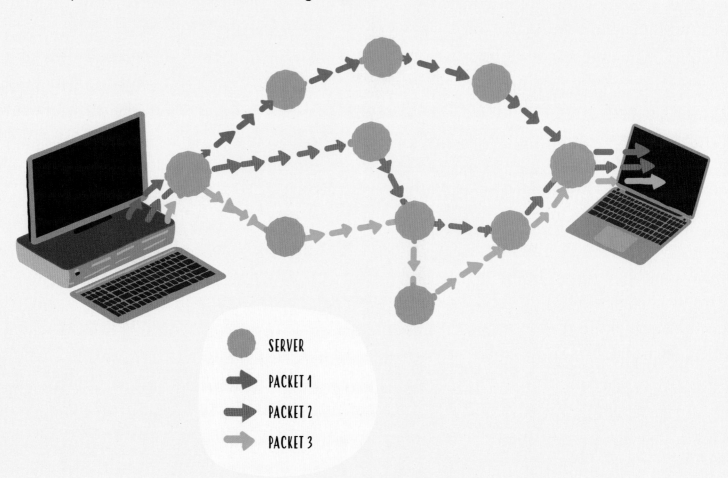

SERVER

PACKET 1

PACKET 2

PACKET 3

IP address
123.45.678.9

Domain
www.url.com

 ## WHERE TO?

The system that moves packets of data around the Internet is called the **Internet Protocol** (IP). Each computer or other device has an Internet Protocol address. Each packet that travels through the Internet is marked with the address of where it's going. The address is made up of four numbers separated by dots. We don't need to know these numbers because we can use addresses made up of words instead, such as www.thisbook.com. These are called domains, and they are automatically changed into numbers by servers on the Internet.

THE CLOUD

People and organizations often store their data on Internet servers instead of on their own computers. This is called "cloud" storage. The data could be photographs or a contacts list, or an organization's sales records. The advantage of this is that the data can be looked at from any device connected to the Internet.

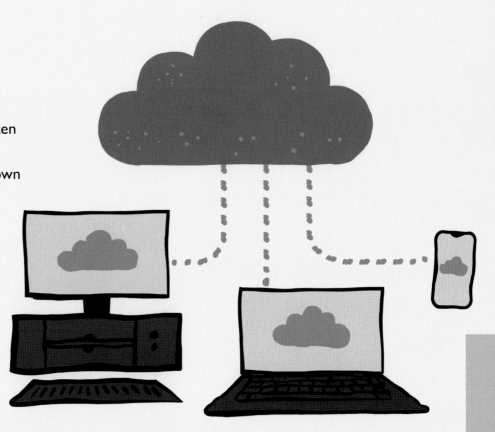

EMAIL

Email is short for electronic mail. An email is a message that's sent electronically over a network (normally the Internet). An email needs to be addressed to the person it's going to, so that it finds its way through the network. The emails you receive are normally stored on a server, and you can view them with an email app.

EMAIL APPS

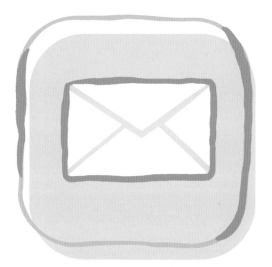

An email app on a computer, tablet, or smartphone is used to compose, send, receive, and manage emails. An email app is sometimes called an email client. The app connects through the Internet to a server where your emails are stored. It displays the messages that are there and allows you to compose new emails and delete old ones. The app checks regularly to see if any new emails have arrived on the server for you.

EMAIL ADDRESSES

If you want to send and receive emails, you need your own email address and an email account that allows you to store your emails on the server of an email "host." An email address has several parts. First is the username, which might be a person's name. Then, there's always an @ sign, which means "at." Finally comes the domain, which is the address of the server on the Internet. The domain is made up of a host name, a dot, and a top-level domain, such as .com or .org.

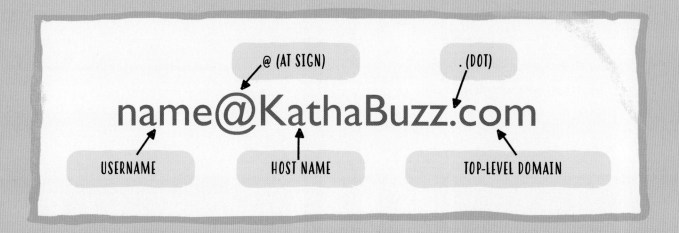

name@KathaBuzz.com

@ (AT SIGN)   . (DOT)

USERNAME   HOST NAME   TOP-LEVEL DOMAIN

EMAIL FOLDERS

Emails are organized into folders called mailboxes. The main folders are:

- An inbox, where emails sent to you are stored

- A sent box, where copies of emails you've sent are stored

- A trash folder, where emails go when you delete them

- A drafts box, where emails you've composed are stored before you send them

- A junk box, where an email app automatically puts emails that it thinks are not important (these are known as spam emails)

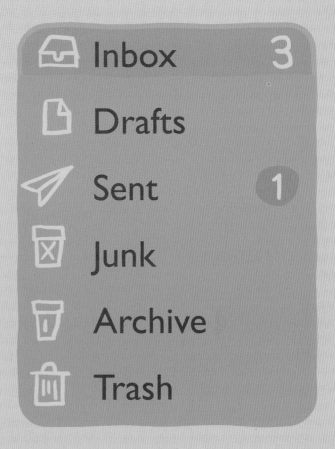

SENDING FILES

As well as the message in an email itself, you can send a file clipped on to the message. The file is called an attachment because it's electronically attached to the message. It might be an image file, a word-processing file, a spreadsheet file, or a pdf document. The size of an attachment is limited to a few megabytes. If you get an email with a paper clip icon on it, this means it has attachment with it.

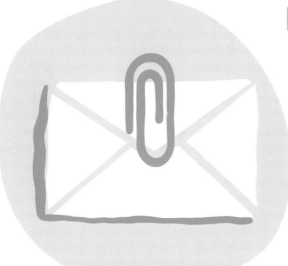

THE WORLD WIDE WEB

The World Wide Web (known as the Web for short) is a collection of millions of websites on the Internet. It lets you look at and download documents, images, videos, and other information; do online shopping and banking; and check social media. To do this, you need a web browser app.

WEB PAGES AND SITES

A typical web page is made up of one or more pages featuring text, pictures, menus, and other items called elements. The pages are connected to each other by links and menus.

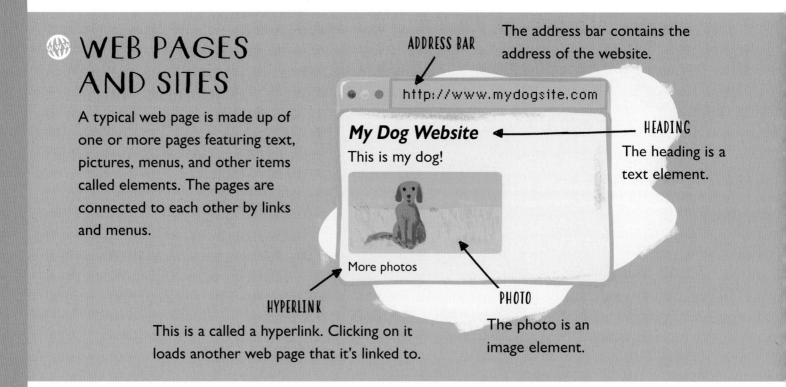

ADDRESS BAR

The address bar contains the address of the website.

http://www.mydogsite.com

HEADING

The heading is a text element.

PHOTO

The photo is an image element.

HYPERLINK

This is a called a hyperlink. Clicking on it loads another web page that it's linked to.

WEB CODE

Web pages are built using a computer language called HyperText Markup Language (HTML). It uses code inside <> symbols to mark headings, images, and hyperlinks. For example, <h1> means a heading, and <p> means a paragraph. This simple HTML is the code for the web page above.

```
<!DOCTYPE html>
<html>
<body>
<h1>My Dog Website</h1>
<p>This is my dog!</p>
<img src='dog.jpeg' />
<p><a href='photos.html'>More photos</a></p>
<body>
</html>
```

<html> tells the computer that the code that follows is in HTML.

<a href= 'photos.html'> tells the computer that the text "More photos" is a link to a web page called photos.html

PARTS OF WEB ADDRESS

Every web page on the Internet has its own address, so that it can be found by computers, tablets, and smartphones that are looking for it. A web address is also called a uniform resource locator (url for short). It always starts with "https://" which means Hypertext Transfer Protocol—that's the way that website data is moved around the Internet. Next comes the domain, which points to the server where the website is stored. Finally, there's the name of a folder where the web page is stored.

OUT OF CURIOSITY

In 2022, there were almost two billion website names registered around the world. Only about 200 million of these are active. On average, 175 new website names are registered every hour.

https://www.mydogsite.com/photos

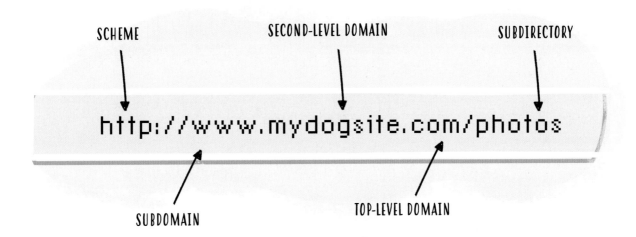

SCHEME SECOND-LEVEL DOMAIN SUBDIRECTORY

http://www.mydogsite.com/photos

SUBDOMAIN TOP-LEVEL DOMAIN

WEB BROWSERS

A web browser is an app that fetches and displays web pages. There are many different browsers, such as MS Edge for Windows, Safari for Mac OS, and Google Chrome. In a browser window, you can enter the address of the web page that you want to visit into the address bar. The browser sends a request to the Internet that finds its way to the server. The server sends the contents of the page back to the browser.

NETWORK DANGERS

There are dangers when your computer or device is connected to the Internet because your machine is connected to millions of the other computers around the world. If you are not careful, these other machines can see what's on your computer, access your online accounts, or damage the computer's software.

MALWARE

Malware is the name given to any software that's designed to do damage to computers. Malware can stop a computer from working by changing its software, stealing its data, or even taking control of it completely, often without the computer owner knowing what's happening. Most computers have software that protects against malware.

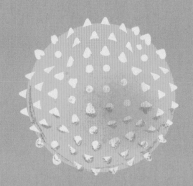

A **virus** might find its way onto your computer if you click on a web-page link or email attachment. It can then spread to another computer inside files or attachments.

A **worm** is a little bit like a virus, but it copies itself and spreads over a network automatically.

Spyware sends information about your computer to another person on the Internet. It can detect key presses on a keyboard, so it might give away your passwords.

🔒 PASSWORDS

We use passwords for many computer activities—for logging on to computers and smartphones, or signing into shopping sites, email, social media, and online bank accounts. Passwords keep other people from pretending to be you. It's risky to use obvious or simple passwords that people could guess. Face recognition and fingerprint recognition also help to keep things secure.

🔒 DATA IN CODE

Sending important or secret data, such as passwords, from one computer to another over a network is risky because somebody might be able to read it. So the data is often turned into code by the computer that sends it. When it arrives at the destination computer, it gets decoded, or decrypted. It can only be decoded by a computer with the right decryption key.

| "PASSWORD123" | ENCRYPTION | "Z0LGRMu+vAX" |

OUT OF CURIOSITY

One of the most damaging viruses was called **ILOVEYOU**, which appeared in the year 2000. Once it got onto a computer, it changed system software and kept the computer from working. It infected 10 million personal computers.

ONLINE SAFETY

The Internet is a fantastic source of information and entertainment, and it's a great way to communicate. But, it can also be a dangerous place. Everyone who goes online needs to protect their privacy by not giving away personal information, by using strong passwords, and by not communicating with strangers.

✅ A DIGITAL FOOTPRINT

Whenever you share a photograph or a video, comment on someone's social media page, click on an ad, or visit a website, you leave a trail of evidence called a digital footprint. Many websites use pieces of code called **cookies** to track what you do on the website. These might reveal which videos you watched or which products you viewed in an online store. People or organizations can track your choices using your footprint. Once you've left a footprint, it's almost impossible to delete it.

✅ SOCIAL MEDIA

Social media has many advantages, including making and talking to friends, sharing photos and videos, making voice and video calls, and writing blogs. But there are disadvantages, too. It's easy to accidentally share too much information with strangers, and people can pretend to be somebody they are not. Some news stories you read on social media are fake, so don't believe everything you read!

✅ SPAM AND PHISHING

A "spam" email is an email from someone you don't know, usually trying to sell you something. Most spam emails don't do any harm, but others might ask you to click on a link or open an attachment. Some spam emails try to trick you into giving away personal information, including bank account information. This is known as **phishing**. Always tell an adult if you receive phishing emails.

✅ CYBERBULLYING

Some people on social media platforms can be abusive to other people online. They think it's okay because nobody knows who they are. Bullying people online is known as cyberbullying. It includes insulting or threatening people on social media or by email or text. Always tell somebody if this happens to you.

"Trolling" is similar. A troll is someone who tries to start arguments by posting comments on social media or forums.

 CHAPTER 6

COMPUTERS EVERYWHERE

When most people hear the word "computer," they imagine
a laptop or desktop computer used at home, school, or work.
They might also think of tablets and smartphones, which are also
computers. As well as these machines, there are computers
hidden away in many other places, working unseen.

This chapter looks at embedded computers that are in machines
from smartwatches to washing machines, as sensors around the home,
in toys and games, in factories, transportation machines,
and even far out in space.

EMBEDDED COMPUTERS

Computers, tablets, and smartphones are not the only machines that contain microprocessors. Other devices do, but we can't change the programs that they run. These microprocessors are known as embedded computers.

MICROPROCESSORS

The microprocessors that are embedded in most devices are smaller and less powerful than those in everyday computers. They usually have simple jobs to do, so speed is not so important. Pictured right is the microprocessor in a smartwatch. The program that controls the watch only changes with a software update. The same program stays running when the machine is switched on.

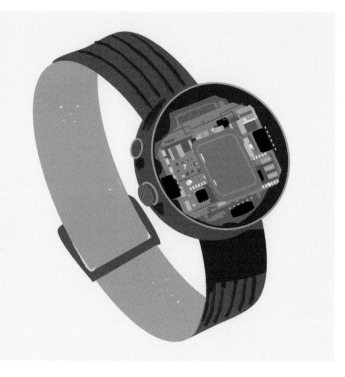

GPS (SATNAV)

An in-car GPS (or satnav) is another device controlled by a microprocessor. Its software figures out your location using a GPS sensor, draws a map of where you are, calculates the best route to a destination, and gives you route directions to follow. The **algorithm** for finding the best route is quite complicated. The map, including data about junctions and local points of interest, is held in a data file and can be updated to include new roads.

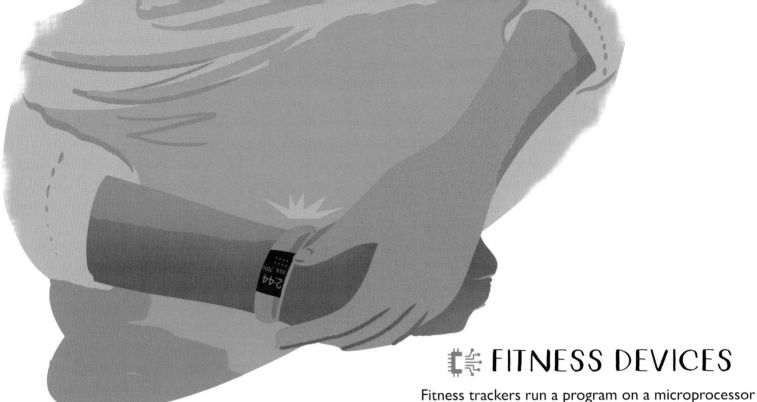

 FITNESS DEVICES

Fitness trackers run a program on a microprocessor that records your activities. A tracker has sensors that detect how your body is moving and your heart rate. Its program uses an algorithm that uses data from the motion sensors to calculate how many steps you have taken or climbed. The same program runs every time you switch on the watch. It records data for each day and displays it on the screen, taking inputs from the buttons.

SMART SPEAKERS

A smart speaker has a microprocessor that runs a program that gives the speaker artificial intelligence (AI). The software recognizes speech and uses the results to do different actions, such as saying the time, playing songs, or doing an Internet search and reading out the results. This gives the impression of an intelligent machine.

SENSORS

Many computerized devices have sensors that pass data to their microprocessor. Sensors can detect the position of a device, temperature, brightness, and sounds, and send digital signals to the processor. The program running in the device decides what actions to take.

WHICH WAY IS UP?

Devices such as games controllers, fitness trackers, and drones have two types of movement sensors: tilt sensors and accelerometers. Tilt sensors detect how much the devices are tilted left, right, forward, or backward. Accelerometers detect when a device starts or stops, speeds up or slows down. A drone's motion sensors send data to the microprocessor, which controls the speed of the propellers to keep the drone flying steadily.

LIGHT OR DARK?

Light sensors detect the amount of light falling on them. Some sensors detect visible light (the light our eyes can detect). A laptop computer uses a light sensor to adjust its screen brightness (brighter for daytime, less bright at night). Some sensors detect infrared light. A robot vacuum cleaner has a proximity sensor to detect obstacles in its way. The sensor sends out a beam of infrared light and detects any light that bounces back. The robot is programmed to turn around when the sensor sends a positive signal.

CODE SCANNERS

A store checkout has a sensor called a barcode reader. It reads the barcode on an item that you are buying. The barcode contains data about the item that's decoded by the scanner and sent to the store's computer. The scanner controls a low-power laser beam that scans backward and forward across the item, detects the light that bounces off, and reads the pattern of black-and-white lines. Barcode scanners are also used in delivery depots, where they read barcodes on packages.

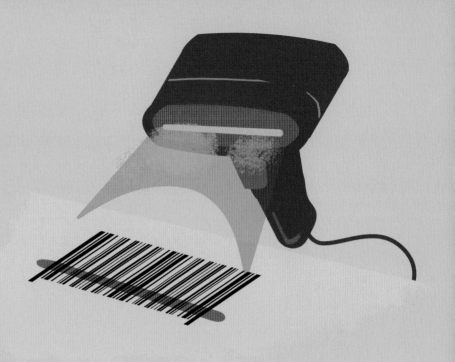

? OUT OF CURIOSITY

Engineers have built walking robots that don't fall over even when they are pushed. These robots' computers take data from onboard motion sensors and calculate which motors to operate to keep the robot upright.

MULTIPLE SENSORS

An automatic weather station has an array of sensors that measure the weather. The sensors turn physical measurements, such as wind speed, into data that is recorded and sent by radio signal to the headquarters of a weather-forecasting service. The sensors include:
• A thermometer to measure temperature
• An anemometer to measure wind strength
• A wind vane to measure wind direction
• A rain gauge to measure rainfall each day
• A hygrometer to measure humidity

MAKING THINGS MOVE

Computer systems can manage lights, motors, and other machinery. For example, the microprocessor in a washing machine controls when the drum motor is running, its speed, and the indicator lights on the control panel. To control machinery, a computer needs an interface that uses data signals to turn electrical circuits on and off.

INDICATOR LIGHTS

Most computer-controlled machines have indicator lights that give us information. These might be simple on/off lights that show which parts of the machine are operating; lights showing the progress of an operation; or fault lights that illuminate when something goes wrong, such as in a car engine management computer. Many machines have small LED displays that give extra information such as the time and speed. All these lights and displays are controlled by the program running on the machine.

SORTING MACHINERY

There are many places where packages and parcels are sorted before they are sent out on delivery trucks. They include distribution warehouses that send goods to stores and customers, container-sorting buildings operated by couriers and postal services, and airport baggage areas. A computer system sorts the items automatically by operating conveyor belts, levers, chutes, and other machinery to send items to the correct place.

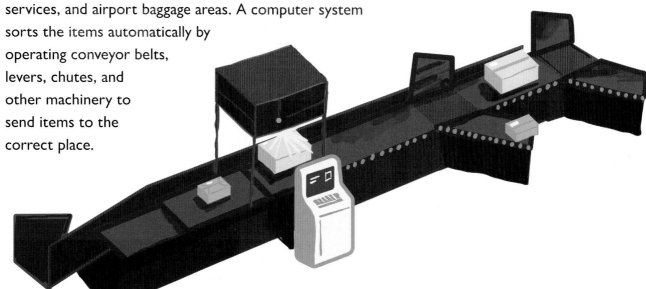

MOTOR CONTROL

A computer can turn a motor on or off and control its speed using an interface. The interface takes data from the computer and uses it to adjust the current flowing to the motor. Devices such as printers, laser cutters, and robots are operated by stepper motors. The speed of a stepper motor is controlled very accurately using data signals. For example, the position of the ink carriage in a printer can be adjusted left or right by tiny amounts.

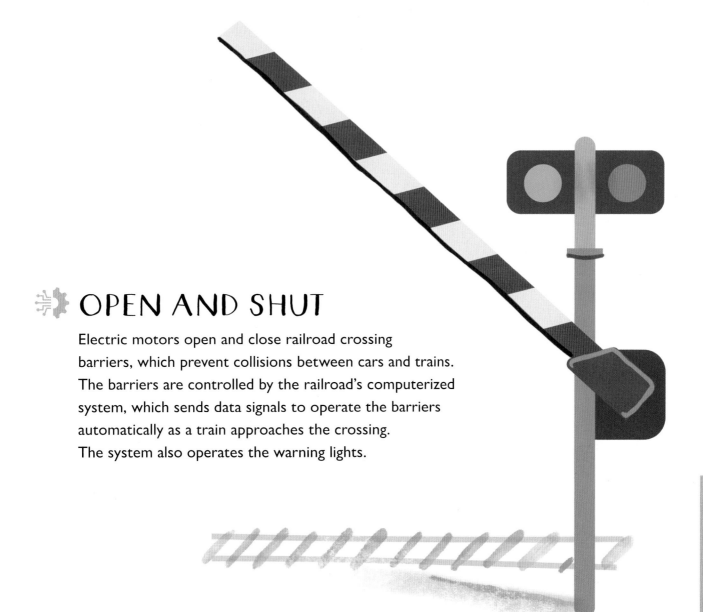

OPEN AND SHUT

Electric motors open and close railroad crossing barriers, which prevent collisions between cars and trains. The barriers are controlled by the railroad's computerized system, which sends data signals to operate the barriers automatically as a train approaches the crossing. The system also operates the warning lights.

DOMESTIC COMPUTERS

Our homes are full of machinery that's operated by embedded computers hidden inside the machines. These machines include washing machines, dishwashers, and central heating systems.

CONTROL BOARDS

In machines, such as washing machines and dishwashers, the electronics that control the machine, including the processor, are all attached to a control board. Information from sensors, such as the water-level sensor in a washing machine drum or the control buttons on a dishwasher, are passed on to the microprocessor, which uses the data to make decisions. It then sends signals to lights, motors, valves, and pumps.

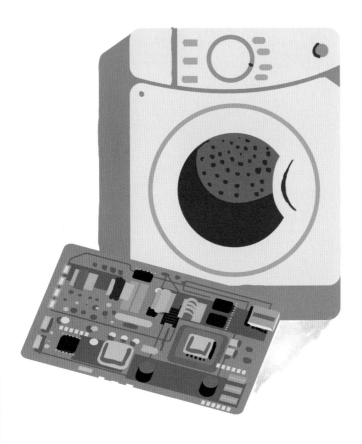

ALARMS

A burglar alarm system is made up of a central control box that's run by a microprocessor, plus sensors that send data to the box. Magnetic sensors detect if doors and windows are open or closed. Infrared sensors detect if a person is moving in a room. Signals are sent to the microprocessor, which decides whether or not to trigger the alarm's lights and sirens. Fire alarms work in a similar way, using heat and smoke detectors.

CHANGING THE FLOW

The control box of a central heating system takes data from temperature sensors and from the program settings stored in it. It decides whether the heating should be on or off and sends signals to the furnace (boiler), telling it to heat water, and to valves and pumps that control the flow of the hot water through pipes and radiators. The control box also detects faults in the system.

SMART APPLIANCES

Some domestic machines are "smart." As well as doing their jobs, such as detecting burglars or washing clothes, they connect to the Internet or to a smartphone. This allows them to be controlled remotely from almost anywhere in the world. A smart refrigerator keeps food cold but also has apps and a Wi-Fi Internet link. It reads the barcodes on items and keeps a list of what you store inside. Recipes from the Internet are displayed on a screen.

OUT OF CURIOSITY

You might have heard of the "Internet of Things." This term is used to mean all the machines that are connected to the Internet, from smartphones and laptops to burglar alarms and smart refrigerators.

TOYS AND GAMES

Many electronic toys contain microprocessors that let users control what actions they take. Computer games can be run on consoles, personal computers, tablets, and smartphones.

COMPUTER GAMES

Games consoles are computers with graphics processors powerful enough to display high-resolution 3D graphics at a high frame rate, which means the graphics move smoothly without jumping. Personal computers designed for gaming also have fast graphics processors, so that they can run 3D games such as flight simulators. A flight simulator application may be controlled by a flight stick, pedals, and levers.

OUT OF CURIOSITY

The speed of a modern games machine is measured in FLOPS, short for floating-point operations per second. These are the calculations needed to display high-speed 3D graphics. The fastest games consoles can manage 12 teraflops (12 trillion FLOPS).

LEARNING TOYS

Computerized toys help children learn about shapes, simple aritmetic, letters of the alphabet, and simple words. A program takes inputs from buttons and a microphone. The program running on the microprocessor chooses how to respond and controls sounds and images on a display. This turtle toy is designed for learning first words.

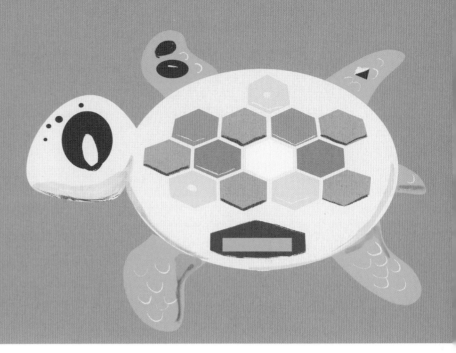

PROGRAMMABLE TOYS

Robotic toys help children take their first steps in programming. This robot is programmed with a block programming language on a smartphone. The final program is transferred to the robot, which then obeys its commands. The robot has touch sensors, a camera, a screen, and motors that move its tracks and arms. It can be programmed to move forward, turn around, pick up objects, produce pictures on its screen, and make sounds.

CHESS GAMES

In a computer chess game, the computer plays chess against you using artificial intelligence. It's a complex programming job to make a computer play a good game of chess. The computer needs to calculate the best move from all the possibilities available. In this game, sensors detect your moves, and lights on each square show which move the computer wants to make.

FACTORY MACHINERY

Computers play a big part in construction in factories. Designers and engineers use computers to design and draw parts for machines such as cars. The components are made using computer-controlled machinery. Robotic machinery also helps to assemble machine parts.

CUTTING COMPUTERS

A milling machine cuts material from a block. It can cut metal, wood, and plastic. Modern milling machines are **computer numerical control** (CNC) machines, which means they have a computer that uses a 3D digital model. They figure out how to remove material to shape an object, then control the cutting head that makes the cuts.

LASER CUTTING

A laser-cutting machine cuts materials such as metal and wood with a high-power laser. An engineer draws the pattern of cuts using an application on a regular computer. The information in the pattern includes the power and speed the laser should use for each cut. The pattern is then sent to the laser machine. A controller in the machine takes data from the pattern, then controls the position and power of the laser to make cuts.

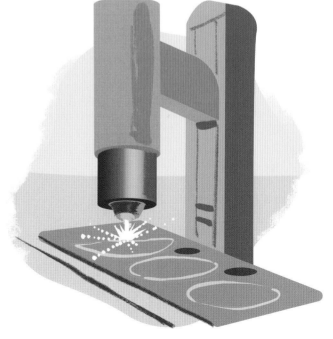

FACTORY ROBOTS

Most of the computer-controlled robots that work in factories are robot arms. The arm has joints and a wrist like a human arm. At the end of the arm is a tool such as a gripper, screwdriver, welding tool, or paint spray gun. The computer is programmed to do a job, such as painting a car body. It calculates how to direct the arm and position the tool for each job.

DELIVERY ROBOTS

Many modern factories use fleets of delivery robots to move parts from one part of the factory to another, such as an assembly line. Each robot has its own computer that guides it around the factory, following tracks on the factory floor. The robot's computer gets instructions from a central computer that tells it what job to do next. The robots return to a charging station when they are not needed.

STORES AND MEDICAL

As well as in homes and factories, computers work in stores and hospitals. We see computers at the checkout when we pay for groceries. In hospitals, computers control diagnostic machines, such as heart monitors and scanners.

STORE COMPUTERS

In a small store, there might be just one checkout, which is a computer itself. It has a barcode scanner to receive information from an item's barcode and a printer to produce payment receipts. In its memory is a database of all the items in the store, their prices, and how many are in stock. In large stores, there are many checkouts connected to a central computer.

VENDING MACHINES

A vending machine is like a mini self-service store. Its operation is controlled by a small computer. A sensor detects when coins are put into the machine. It sends data to the microprocessor, which adds up the value of the coins and sends that to the display. Then, it takes input from the keypad as the person chooses what to buy. Finally, it operates the mechanics that move the item into the dispenser.

🧺 CHARGING STATIONS

Electric vehicles (EVs) have large rechargeable batteries that provide the electricity for their motors. When the batteries are running low, drivers can recharge them at public recharging points. A recharging station is controlled by a computer that carefully controls the flow of electricity to the car. An electric vehicle also has an onboard computer that manages the flow of electricity from the batteries to the motor, making the most efficient use of it.

🧺 EMERGENCY RESPONSE

A defibrillator is a "smart" medical device. It is used in an emergency to help a person whose heart has stopped beating or is beating irregularly. When the machine is switched on, it runs a program that tells the person operating it what to do, using lights and sounds. It detects how the patient's heart is beating and then triggers an electric shock to try and return the heart to its correct rhythm.

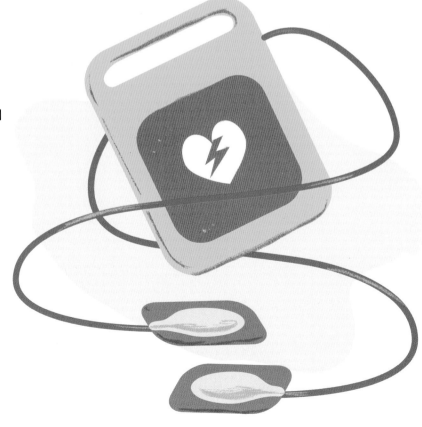

TRANSPORTATION

Computers are vital for transporting us from place to place. They work in cars, trains, ships, and aircraft, helping drivers, pilots, and navigators keep on course and check how their machines are running. They also control traffic on the ground and in the air, helping to keep passengers safe.

AUTOPILOT

Most of the time that a passenger plane is in the air, it's being flown by an autopilot—a computer system that steers it through the air. Modern airliners are controlled by computers even when the pilot is in control. The computer takes inputs from the pilot's flying controls (stick, pedals, and thrust levers), and decides how to move the plane's flight surfaces (ailerons, rudder, and elevators) and how much power to use to steer the plane. This is known as a "fly-by-wire" system.

COMPUTER BOOKINGS

Airlines operate computer systems that keep track of the passengers booked on a flight. The system creates a database of the passengers' names, passport information, and seat numbers when the passenger makes a booking. When a passenger arrives at the airport to check in, the system updates the database to list the passengers boarding. Computer systems also keep track of passengers' baggage to make sure it reaches the right plane.

TRAFFIC CONTROL

Computer systems control the timing of traffic signals at busy intersections. Sensors detect approaching traffic, and a program makes decisions about when to change the lights to keep the traffic moving. In cities, the systems are linked together, so that traffic moves smoothly from one intersection to the next. Air traffic controllers (ATC) rely on computers that collect data from aircraft, display it on maps, and give warnings about possible collisions. On railroads, computers operate signals to prevent two trains from being on the same section of track.

AVOIDING HAZARDS

Ships have navigation systems that are like the GPS systems in a car. A system displays a nautical chart showing the position of the ship and the sea around it. It shows the depth of water, land, underwater hazards such as rocks and wrecks, and buoys that show safe channels for ships to take. On larger ships, an autopilot can steer the ship and control its speed.

24° 26.1981 N   118° 10.3610'E

THE RISE AND RISE OF COMPUTERS

The first electronic computers were invented less than 100 years ago. They were incredible for the time but were very slow even compared to a modern smartphone. They were also rare and expensive. Today, billions of people have their own computers and use them daily. People are finding more and more ways to use computers, and new apps appear all the time.

DISTANT COMPUTERS

Computers haven't just spread all over our planet—they have made it into space, too! Robotic space probes carry computers that guide them, operate their sensors, and send data back to scientists on Earth. NASA's Perseverance rover landed on Mars in 2021. Its job is to look for evidence of ancient life on the planet. Perseverance is controlled by a computer designed to survive the violent vibrations during its launch from Earth and landing on Mars.

OUT OF CURIOSITY

The computer that's farthest from home is aboard the Voyager 1 probe, which left Earth in 1977 to explore the outer solar system. Voyager 1 is now billions of miles from Earth. Its computer, which has just 70 kilobytes of memory, is still working.

ON ITS OWN

Mars is so far from Earth that it takes up to 20 minutes for radio signals to travel from Mars to Earth and back. This makes it impossible for an Earth operator to steer Perseverance across the Martian surface. Instead, the onboard computer does the driving, sensing, and avoiding any Martian boulder that might be in its way.